THE INVISIBILITY FACTOR

THE INVISIBILITY FACTOR

ADMINISTRATORS AND FACULTY
REACH OUT TO FIRST-GENERATION
COLLEGE STUDENTS

Edited by

TERESA HEINZ HOUSEL
&
VICKIE L. HARVEY

BrownWalker Press
Boca Raton

The Invisibility Factor:
Administrators and Faculty Reach Out to First-Generation College Students

BrownWalker Press
Boca Raton, Florida • USA
2009

ISBN-10: 1-59942-523-8 (paper)
ISBN-13: 978-1-59942-523-8 (paper)

ISBN-10: 1-59942-524-6 (ebook)
ISBN-13: 978-1-59942-524-5 (ebook)

www.brownwalker.com

Library of Congress Cataloging-in-Publication Data

The invisibility factor : administrators and faculty reach out to first-
generation college students / edited by Teresa Heinz Housel, Vickie
L. Harvey.
    p. cm.
Includes bibliographical references.
ISBN-13: 978-1-59942-523-8 (pbk. : alk. paper)
ISBN-10: 1-59942-523-8 (pbk. : alk. paper)
    1. First-generation college students--United States. 2. People with
social disabilities--Education (Higher)--United States. I. Housel,
Teresa Heinz, 1972- II. Harvey, Vickie L., 1956-
LC4069.6.I58 2009
378.1'982694--dc22

                                                    2009045509

✦ TABLE OF CONTENTS ✦

FOREWORD
Administrators and Faculty Reach Out to First-Generation
College Students
Melissa Ballard VII

SECTION I
INTRODUCTION AND PEDAGOGICAL FOUNDATIONS 11

CHAPTER ONE
Introduction and Overview of Book's Objectives
Teresa Heinz Housel and Vickie L. Harvey 13

CHAPTER TWO
Guiding Class Consciousness in First-Generation
College Students: A Pragmatic Approach to Classism
in the Academy
Brandi Lawless 23

CHAPTER THREE
Until Mr. Right Comes Along: Social Mobility,
Higher Education, and the Lure of Cultural Elitism
JoAnne M. Podis 35

SECTION II
MEETING THE CHALLENGES OF FIRST-GENERATION
STUDENTS THROUGH ACADEMIC PROGRAMS 45

CHAPTER FOUR
The Role of Generational Status, Program Affiliation,
and Cultural Background in the Performance of
College Students
Alice Araujo and Andreas Anastasiou 47

CHAPTER FIVE
Humble and Hopeful: Welcoming First-Generation
Poor and Working-Class Students to College
Kenneth Oldfield 59

CHAPTER SIX
Understanding the Impacts of Socioeconomic Status
on First-Generation Students: A Case Study
Harmony Paulsen and Jena Griswold 75

CHAPTER SEVEN
Opportunities and Challenges in a University-Level
Program for First-Generation Students
Keith Nainby 91

CHAPTER EIGHT
Creating Living and Learning Communities that
Engage Our First-Generation Students:
Suggestions for Policy and Practice
Rita L. Rahoi-Gilchrest, Sarah Olcott, and Ron Elcombe 101

CHAPTER NINE
The Nine Needs of Lower-Income,
First-Generation College Students
Charlie Johnson 125

CHAPTER TEN
Conclusions
Vickie Harvey and Teresa Heinz Housel 141

AUTHOR INFORMATION
Our Qualifications for Editing this Book 145
Primary Editors 149
Authors and Contributors 151

◆ FOREWORD ◆
ADMINISTRATORS AND FACULTY REACH OUT TO FIRST-GENERATION COLLEGE STUDENTS

Melissa Ballard

At extended family gatherings when I was a young adult, my dad would often call to me across the room. "Hey, Melissa, you went to college." This was a noteworthy comment because I was the first in my family to do so. After the silence that inevitably followed, he asked me to verify an obscure fact or come up with the answer to a question unrelated to my field of study. I think he did it partly to brag, but also to remind me that I still didn't know everything. At some level I'm sure he wondered if the cost and time involved in my liberal arts education were worth it.

During my college days, I never thought about the fact that I was a first-generation student. In part, this might have been because I attended a large state school where the background of many of the students was similar to my own. But I do remember, vividly, talking to students who were mysteriously knowledgeable about scholarships, grants, internships, how to effectively communicate with professors, and how to study efficiently while making it all look easy. I knew none of these things. In fact, until I began to work in Student Academic Services at Oberlin College some fourteen years ago, and learned that we provide focused services to students who are first-generation, I was not even aware of the term.

Working in student support services at a small liberal arts college, I have seen over and over again how vital it is for first-generation students to have support as they, literally, work their way through college. We offer academic success workshops; credit-bearing courses in study and reading strategies, mathematics and communication skills; and individual tutoring. While these services are available to all students, an additional effort is made to reach out to first-generation students in the form of special advising (one-on-one meetings with staff members to discuss a variety of issues related to academics and general well-being) and a peer-mentoring program. Our first-generation students seem to be extremely mature and capable, but they very much benefit from having people who will listen to their stories, understand their unique challenges, and guide them through the sometimes mysterious, confusing, and intimidating halls of academe.

In May of 2006, I felt as though I had come full circle when I sat on Oberlin College's Commencement platform in my role of class dean for the seniors. It was one of the hottest, most humid May days on record for Northeast Ohio—not the ideal time to be wearing a long, scratchy, black robe. The heat was worth it, though, to watch the Class of 2006—which included my daughter—walk across the stage to accept their diplomas. I knew most of the students, including many who were first-generation. I also knew some of their struggles, in part because they were once my own: family members who wonder aloud when they will get a "real" job, constant money worries, and the feeling of always being unprepared when compared to one's peers. But I also knew that as those graduates walked off that stage, they felt exultant. And I believe their education will lead them to yet unimagined people, places, and rich experiences, as mine has done for me.

While sitting on that stage, and in spare moments since, I've reflected on the ways in which my work has been informed by the expertise of my colleagues and the student mentors who work in our department; many of them are first-generation. I have also been able to draw on my own college experiences, uninformed as they were at the time. In terms of written material, I have found many helpful resources, but no single volume that could serve as a comprehensive reference for working with first-generation students.

I am, therefore, extremely pleased to be introducing this book. The authors represent faculty and staff, many of them former first-generation students, as well as current students. I'm convinced that *The Invisibility Factor: Administrators and Faculty Reach Out to First-Generation College Students* will quickly become an essential resource for college personnel, as it contains both a thorough examination of issues faced by first-generation students in the academy and a myriad of practical, research-based suggestions for meeting those needs through teaching, programming, and individual support.

In Section I (Chapters 1-3), Chapter 1 the editors provide an overview of the first-generation student population, a brief literature review that addresses potential obstacles for students, and a discussion of the scope and purpose of the book. Chapters 2 and 3 include specific suggestions for supporting first-generation students in the classroom while also addressing issues of social class. In Section II (Chapters 4 through 10) readers are offered multiple approaches to providing institutional support for first-generation students as they attempt to acclimate academically, socially, and personally to the culture of the academy. This section includes descriptions of specific programs, including peer mentoring. Chapter 10 summarizes the book's content and makes additional recommendations for providing effective first-generation services. Personal narratives form a thread that is woven throughout the text, clarifying and enriching the theories and proposals that are outlined.

When Teresa and Vickie invited me to write this foreword, I had what might be considered a typical first-generation reaction: I was simultaneously thrilled and horrified. Me? Write something for a scholarly text? Despite having worked in higher education for many years, part of me will always feel like something of an outsider. But my education continues to afford me new and exciting opportunities, and this is one of them. So, when I look back on my dad's unstated question my answer is, "Yes, Dad, I went to college. And it *was* worth it." This book will assist all of us in guiding first-generation students on this most worthwhile of journeys.

Melissa Ballard
Oberlin, Ohio
September 2009

Portions of this foreword appeared in the Summer 2006 edition of the *Oberlin Alumni Magazine*.

◆ SECTION I ◆

INTRODUCTION AND PEDAGOGICAL FOUNDATIONS

◆ CHAPTER ONE ◆
INTRODUCTION AND OVERVIEW OF BOOK'S OBJECTIVES

Teresa Heinz Housel and Vickie L. Harvey

This book responds to an increasing student population that is all too often underserved and unrecognized. First-generation students (or FGS, whose parents do not have a bachelor's or an associate degree) are enrolling at American colleges and universities at steadily increasing rates. According to a 2007 study by the University of California-Los Angeles's Higher Education Research Institute, nearly one in six freshmen at American four-year institutions are FGS (Saenz, Hurtado, Barrera, Wolf & Yeung, 2007).

The efforts of institutions to recruit more low-income students (who are often first-generation) represent part of this enrollment increase. As the number of first-generation applicants to higher education institutions increases, institutions face public criticism about rising tuition costs and questions about accessibility for low-income students.

In December 2007, Harvard University, which has a $35 billion endowment, announced it would replace student loans with grants for families earning less than $180,000 a year (Kinzie, 2007, p. A08). The new program ensures that students from families earning less than $60,000 a year would likely pay nothing to attend Harvard. According to Jan's (2009) *Boston Globe* article, "The Harvard Disadvantage," about the university's financial aid initiative, the number of Harvard students from families with annual incomes below $60,000 has risen 30 percent (or one-fifth of all Harvard students) during the past five years (p. 1).

Similar to the Harvard initiative, Oberlin College announced its new Oberlin Access Initiative program in April 2008. The program replaces student loans with grants for incoming first-year students eligible for federally funded Pell Grants. The program will also eliminate loans for current, Pell-eligible students at Oberlin. These students often come from families earning less than $35,000 annually (Bader, 2008, p. 14). Describing the new program, Oberlin College President Marvin Krislov said, "There has been a sea change in the way colleges are thinking about financial aid. Access has become a major public policy issue" (Bader, p. 12). The financial aid initiatives operated by Harvard and other institutions underscore the almost absolute necessity for a college degree in today's economic climate.

Not Just Access:
Barriers to Success for First-Generation College Students
Today's students are up against an economic downfall in which employers can demand that new hires have a bachelor's degree. It is not necessarily that employers value what the student learned, just that the student has a degree. For potential employees, the college degree is a no-cost screening device for detecting the bright and ambitious who have perseverance and would make better employees. The more people who go to college, the more it makes sense for employers to require a college degree. However, where does this leave the FGS if they are to stay marketable and dare we add, educated?

Although financial aid programs help level out unequal access to higher education, the programs are just part of the overall equation because many FGS face additional barriers to academic success when they enter an unfamiliar academic culture. To help FGS better culturally adapt to the campus environment, Harvard recently began initiatives such as a fund to help such students pay for incidental expenses for social activities, clothes, and travel home. Although first-generation Harvard students might feel intellectually comfortable, students interviewed by Jan (2009) describe the "minefield of class chasms on a campus still brimming with legacies and wealth" (p. 1). Jan discussed the university's difficulty of identifying the neediest students because some are embarrassed to reveal their socioeconomic circumstances.

Of course, the specific difficulties experienced by FGS are nuanced depending on their campus environments, which widely range across private liberal arts colleges, community colleges, and large universities in urban and rural settings. However, education researchers document how FGS enter college with more potential barriers to achievement than non-FGS. Researchers identify how FGS frequently lack reading, writing, and oral communication skills, which can translate into poor retention rates (Ryan & Glenn, 2002/2003; Reid & Moore, 2008). Other studies indicate that FGS take part in fewer extracurricular organizations, campus cultural programs, internships, and career networking activities than their peers from middle- and upper-class economic backgrounds (Glenn, 2004; Moschetti & Hudley, 2008). Additionally, FGS typically have lower levels of parental involvement in their education and they carry the burden of financial worries (McCarron & Inkelas, 2006; Bui, 2002).

Moreover, many FGS feel socially, ethnically, and emotionally marginalized on campus (Francis & Miller, 2008; Bui, 2002; Lundberg, Schreiner, Hovaguimian & Miller, 2007). These challenges are usually the most difficult for institutions to identify because they typically result from unspoken cultural expectations and social mores. FGS often lack social capital, such as overseas travel and exposure to cultural arts that wealthier students might take for granted. FGS must often navigate the unwritten social rules of their peers, professors, and academic administrators, many of whom come from middle- and upper-class backgrounds (Lubrano, 2004).

Struggles That Have No Boundaries:
Two Famous First-Generation Students
Examples from the experiences of two famous public figures, who were also FGS, especially confirm how these students face common academic and emotional struggles.

Shortly after U.S. President Barack Obama nominated Sonia Sotomayor as a Supreme Court Justice in May 2009, *The New York Times* printed a lengthy feature that traced Sotomayor's journey from the East Bronx projects to her climb up the legislative ladder as attorney and judge.

Stolberg's (2009) *New York Times* article poignantly noted Sotomayor's college experience at Princeton, where she was a history major in the 1970s. Kenneth K. Roy, a childhood friend who encouraged Sotomayor to attend Princeton, gave her a warning about what to expect at the elite institution: "'I told her I don't want you to come here with any illusions. Social isolation is going to be a part of your experience, and you have to have the strength of character to get through that'" (Stolberg, p. A18)

When Sotomayor began college classes in the fall of 1972, she was outnumbered in both ethnicity and gender. Although she had been valedictorian of her larger urban high school, she described the feeling of being suddenly out of place among her classmates. According to Stolberg's (2009) article, Sotomayor confessed to a Yale Law School friend that "she could 'barely write' when she arrived at Princeton'" (p. A18). She rarely raised her hand in class discussions and spent summers "inhaling children's classics, grammar books and literature that many Princeton peers had already conquered at Choate or Exeter" (Stolberg, p. A18).

Sotomayor's college experience resonates with those of Hillary Rodham Clinton, U.S. Secretary of State and former presidential candidate. In her autobiography, *Living History* (2003), Clinton recounts the day her parents dropped her off at Wellesley College. "I arrived at Wellesley carrying my father's political beliefs and my mother's dreams and left with the beginnings of my own," recounts Clinton. "But on that first day, as my parents drove away, I felt lonely, overwhelmed and out of place" among students who had attended private boarding schools, traveled abroad, and spoke other languages (p. 27).

Similar to other FGS, Clinton initially struggled in her college courses. As she recalls, "I didn't hit my stride as a Wellesley student right away" (Clinton, 2003, p. 27). After a month of school, Clinton phoned home and told her parents that she was not smart enough to be there. Clinton's father, Hugh Rodham, said that she could come home while her mother, Dorothy, insisted that she not give up. Clinton took her mother's advice: "After a shaky start, the doubts faded, and I realized that I really couldn't go home again, so I might as well make a go of it" (Clinton, p. 28).

It was only several months later, during the winter, when Clinton (2003) realized that she was going to survive at Wellesley. The college president, Margaret Clapp, visited Clinton's dorm and invited her and other students to shake the snow off nearby trees so the branches wouldn't break under the snow's weight. "We walked from tree to tree through knee-high snow under a clear sky filled with stars, led by a strong, intelligent woman alert to the surprises and vulnerabilities of nature," remembers Clinton. "I decided that night that I had found the place where I belonged" (p. 28).

Sotomayor, Clinton, this volume's co-editors, and many chapter authors navigated the unfamiliar social codes and academic requirements of college. We managed through sheer hard work and courage. Once we found our footing, we asked questions and created our own support networks independent of our families who could not always give us the type of advice we needed. Like many FGS, we may have lacked college preparation, but we possessed survival skills in spades.

Research Informed by Experience: Scholars as FGS Students

Experiences of survival and cultural transition motivate many of this book's contributing authors, who bring important personal and scholarly expertise to their work. The authors include faculty, administrators, support services personnel, and former students at private liberal arts colleges, major research universities, community colleges, and comprehensive universities in urban and rural settings. The diverse perspectives represented in the essays will benefit administrators and staff working at diverse types of institutions with FGS.

Socio-economic background profoundly shapes a person's cultural transition into college and heavily determines what barriers to academic success he or she will face. Many authors in this collection were FGS who made the transition into a foreign academic culture. This book's co-editors, Vickie Harvey and Teresa Heinz Housel, begin by briefly describing our experiences at two very different academic institutions, which nonetheless presented us with distinct social, economic, and academic challenges common to FGS.

Vickie Harvey

I remember being 26 years old and having a conversation with my best friend that changed the trajectory of my life.

Paula: "What are you doing this afternoon?"
Me: "Nothing."
Paula: "Come to class with me. My women's studies teacher is really cool and we talk about great stuff."
Me: "Are you allowed to bring someone to class?"
Paula: "Sure."
Me: "Okay."

Hence began my love of academic learning. I didn't enroll the same day I visited her class because I had to wait for that semester to end and the next to begin. At age 27, I took my first college course and in four years earned my B.A. I continued on for my master's and debated going the final step to earn a Ph.D. My mother said, "There's more? I thought you already had your degree? There's another degree you need to be a teacher?"

Yes, I am a first-generation college student and I am finishing my 19th year of teaching college. I am proud to have returned to college at age 27 as a nontraditional FGS and continued until I earned enough degrees to become a teacher (as my mother would say).

Teresa Heinz Housel

Even though my immediate family environment was not conducive to attending college, I always gravitated toward learning. As a child I spent hours looking at world maps and reading encyclopedias, imagining the places I would explore. My innate desire to learn set me apart from my peers at a rural public school. Similar to many other children in this situation, I was socially ostracized, and that experience later fueled my interest in cultural studies and passionate activist spirit on behalf of people who are silenced.

I knew from the many books that I read that there was a much larger world beyond the one where I grew up. That awareness led me to Oberlin College, where I finally was surrounded by other young people who shared my love for learning. However, in college I sometimes experienced a nameless anxiety. My wealthier classmates all seemed to have assumed experiences such as international travel, knowledge of the fine arts, and prep school educations.

Even though I was bright, I struggled to catch up academically with my peers during my first year of college. The experience perplexed and frustrated me because I studied diligently. To describe just a couple examples, I had long enjoyed my high school history classes, but I was stunned to receive a C- on my first college history essay exam. In my rural high school, where history classes were usually taught by the school's athletic director with little or no historical training, I had learned history only as memorized facts, not as a narrative with varying conflicts and themes. I performed similarly in my college English classes even though I always loved writing. In high school I had learned to follow a formulaic essay outline, but I did not know how to interrogate ideas in a text.

Even though I criticized myself at the time for just not trying hard enough, I now know that my emotional and academic struggles are common to FGS.

How This Book Came to Be

What made us take on the exhilarating and difficult effort of co-editing a book on first-generation college students? Our impetus came from two different directions: first, from our personal standpoint, and second, because of a professional need.

We met many years ago at the National Communication Association's annual convention. We both belonged to the Undergraduate College and University Section, which is a smaller unit of the larger association. Several years ago, Teresa posted a call for book chapters on FGS. Through our ensuing conversations, we eventually became friends and learned we were both first-generation college students. That commonality eventually brought us to work together as co-editors.

The book's second motivation came from the frustration experienced by both our colleagues and ourselves as we worked with FGS. The large number of college courses focusing on race, gender, sexuality, and ethnicity reflect how these constructs are recognized by academics as important aspects of human identity. Far fewer courses address social class in the United States and elsewhere. Still, even at a time when scholars from different disciplines are giving slightly more attention to class, there is no collective resource for support staff and faculty who work with FGS.

Additionally, we consistently heard from colleagues that the literature on first-generation college students included personal narratives, literature reviews, or out-of-date scholarship. There are also few qualitative and quantitative studies on FGS. Personal narratives are certainly a useful starting point for understanding what specific struggles FGS face, and the authors touch on their personal experiences as first-generation college students throughout this book. However, this book combines narrative essays with updated scholarly investigation of how FGS cope with and experience academic culture. The essays collectively represent a balance of personal narrative, qualitative, and quantitative approaches. Taken together, both personal narratives and scholarly writing give readers a holistic perspective on how they can assist FGS in unique ways that address their particular struggles. We knew there was a great need for a readable and practical book offering a combination of methodologies with recommendations that appeal to staff, faculty, and administrators who work with FGS.

Therefore, this collective volume fills an important gap in first-generation research by simultaneously achieving important goals.

The essays review the existing literature on FGS; outline the barriers to college success faced by FGS; update the existing literature by introducing new and cutting-edge first-generation research; and recommend solutions to those in the trenches, who include support staff who design programs to support FGS and faculty who teach and learn from FGS.

This edited volume is primarily tailored to faculty development centers. The spirit of faculty development manifests itself throughout colleges and universities that create and sustain programs geared toward supporting FGS. There are existing practices and programs that are coordinated through faculty development programs such as teaching and learning workshops, faculty development conferences, new faculty orientation, and new student and transfer student orientations.

There are other successful programs not affiliated with faculty development centers that also promote opportunities for faculty who work directly with FGS. Such programs include first-generation programs, first year programs, nontraditional student programs, summer reading programs, faculty-student mentoring, tutoring programs, and honors programs, to identify a few. The names of the programs vary from college to college, but ultimately they are carefully designed to meet the changing needs of more and more FGS who enter our doors. These formal and sometimes less formal venues provide faculty with the needed resources for FGS success.

We believe that the degree of success that FGS experience in colleges and universities is directly linked to the instructional and evaluative resources available to the teaching faculty through the programs identified above. Above all else, this book is intended to be used in these programs to help create an environment conducive to growth, revitalization and renewal for staff and faculty, and ultimately the academic and professional success of FGS.

Book Overview and Themes

The book is organized into two sections:

Section I, "Introduction and Overview of Book's Objectives," examines class's contextual influence on academic performance and cultural transition, the challenges of teaching first-generation college students, and outlines concrete pedagogical strategies for creating respectful, collaborative, and productive learning environments.

Section II, "Meeting the Challenges of First-Generation Students through Academic Programs," focuses on specific and creative ways in which universities and colleges can improve institutional, social, and academic support for FGS.

The book's essays collectively address the following topics of concern to administrators, faculty and staff who interact with FGS:

- Balancing home and academic cultures
- Understanding classism in the academy and class segregation on campus
- Effective pedagogy for teaching FGS
- Race, ethnicity, class, and immigration as they impact FGS' campus experiences
- Insight for developing successful first-generation support service programs
- FGS' emotional, academic, and cultural adjustment to campus life
- Balancing work and financial struggles with college studies
- Instructors' classroom challenges of dealing with respect and authority with FGS
- The impact of a FGS' living situation (such as in a campus living-learning center) on academic and cultural transition

This book will ultimately benefit students by helping administrators, faculty and staff better understand how to reach out to FGS. These students bring an important but underrepresented perspective into academia. By recognizing contextual factors such as class on students' academic performance and cultural transition into college, colleges and universities can create campus environments that are appreciative and respectful of everyone. Many FGS already possess survival skills that give them the courage to forge the unfamiliar college path. However, faculty, staff, and administrators can work together to help even more FGS create stories of success.

References

Bader, R. (2008). A question of access. *Oberlin Alumni Magazine, 103*(4), 12-17.

Bui, K. V. (2002). First-generation college students at a four-year university: Background characteristics, reasons for pursuing higher education, and first-year experiences. *College Student Journal, 36*(1), 3-11.

Clinton, H. R. (2003). *Living history.* New York: Simon & Schuster.

Francis, T. A., & Miller, M. T. (2008). Communication apprehesion: Levels of first-generation college students at 2-year institutions. *Community College Journal of Research and Practice, 32*(1), 38-55.

Glenn, D. (2004, September 3). For needy students, college success depends on more than access, study finds. *The Chronicle of Higher Education, 51*(2), p. A41.

Jan, T. (2009, May 12). The Harvard disadvantage. *The Boston Globe,* p. 1.

Kinzie, S. (2007, December 12). Other colleges eye Harvard's plan to increase affordability. *The Washington Post,* p. A08.

Lubrano, A. (2004). *Limbo: Blue-collar roots, white-collar dreams.* Hoboken, NJ: John Wiley & Sons.

Lundberg, C. A., Schreiner, L. A., Hovaguimian, K., & Miller, S. S. (2007). First-generation status and student race/ethnicity as district predictors of student involvement and learning. *NASPA Journal (Online), 44*(1), 57-83.

McCarron, G. P., & Inkelas, K. K. (2006). The gap between educational aspirations and attainment for first-generation college students and the role of parental involvement. *Journal of College Student Development, 47*(5), 534-549.

Moschetti, R., & Hudley, C. (2008). Measuring social capital among first-generation and non-first-generation, working-class, white males. *Journal of College Admission, 198*(Winter 2008), 25-30.

Reid, M. J., & Moore, J. L. (2008). College readiness and academic preparation for postsecondary education: Oral histories of first-generation urban college students. *Urban Education, 43*(2), 240-261.

Ryan, M. P., & Glenn, P. A. (2002/2003). Increasing one-year retention rates by focusing on academic competence: An empirical odyssey. *Journal of College Student Retention, 4*(3), 297-324.

Saenz, V. B., Hurtado, S., Barrera, D., Wolf, D., & Yeung, F. (2007). *First in my family: A profile of first-generation college students at four-year institutions since 1971.* Los Angeles: Higher Education Research Institute.

Stolberg, S. G. (2009, May 27). A trailblazer and a dreamer. *The New York Times,* p. A1.

◆ CHAPTER TWO ◆
GUIDING CLASS CONSCIOUSNESS IN FIRST-GENERATION COLLEGE STUDENTS: A PRAGMATIC APPROACH TO CLASSISM IN THE ACADEMY

Brandi Lawless

Many FGS struggle with transitioning to college from high school. When I went to college, I was nervous and excited about the social, economic, and academic challenges I would face. I did not expect that some people on campus would think I did not belong there. Responding to my first writing assignment, my freshman English composition instructor told me that I lacked the vocabulary necessary for college success. I was confused about how my professor could strongly question my intelligence. After all, my high school assistant principal had written in a recommendation, "I do not see Brandi stopping at less than a Master's degree." Why, then, was my success potential being challenged? It took me a long time to understand that the problem stemmed from the differences between where I had come from (a small town in rural Pennsylvania) and where I had gone (a highly populated, high-class institution).

Reflecting on my experience, it becomes painfully obvious that the language I used and the lower-class experiences I brought to college were labeled as inferior to those other students. I felt like I did not belong unless I altered my behavior. Stories like mine are not uncommon. hooks (2000) states, "Throughout my graduate student years, I was told again and again that I lacked the proper decorum of a graduate student, that I did not understand my place. Slowly, I began to understand fully that there was no place in academe for folks from working-class backgrounds who did not wish to leave the past behind" (p. 42).

Though many FGS may not identify as lower or working class, the National Center for Educational Statistics (2005) reports that compared to peers whose parents have college degrees, FGS are more likely to be Black or Hispanic or come from low-income families (p. 7). In fact, more than 50 percent of FGS have families with incomes below the poverty line, and an additional 34 percent can be labeled "low income" (NCES, 2005).

Scholars document class consciousness and classism in higher education. Some argue that the university maintains social class order by marginalizing students from lower- and working-class backgrounds (Engen, 2004; hooks, 2000; Moon, 2001; Wong(Lau), 2004). Both Wong(Lau) and hooks describe their felt need to erase their class origins and other interrelated parts of their identity (such as race, ethnicity, and gender) if they wanted to "belong" in the academy.

Engen (2004) describes how a change in world view often accompanies transition into college and disrupts identity. The values and expectations of a lower- or working-class person's home life usually differ from those of their middle-class peers and professors. These changes in world view and self-identity can invalidate a person, make him or her rebellious, or motivate change, as in my case. In other words, the college setting motivates some FGS to change class identity. Cabrera and Padilla (2004) examine class consciousness in their case study of two Mexican FGS. They found that these students transitioned into the middle-class college culture to achieve academic success (p. 154). This culture is taken for granted by middle-class families and remains a barrier for lower-class families with little or no education (Cabrera & Padilla, p. 153).

Reconstructing class identity is not easy because the criteria for class identity are usually implicit. A lower- or working-class student may not understand the implicit behavioral expectations of academic culture. This chapter examines why instructors must expose the invisible expectations they have of students and re-evaluate how they perpetuate these normalized expectations in the classroom. I introduce ideas for integrating class into the curriculum in order to recognize social biases and reduce the culture shock that FGS often experience.

Social Class in the Lives of FGS
Class systems have existed for centuries. The word "class" comes from the Roman word classis, or a system used to separate people

into groups in order to tax them (Allen, 2004). Karl Marx defines class in terms of social relationships and connection to the economic process, rather than societal rank (Lee & Paek, 2005). Max Weber claimed that people are segregated into class categories based on property, prestige, and power (Fussell, 1983).

The definition of class has continually shifted. Some scholars denote class as connected to capital, or the amount of assets and resources one possesses (Bradley & Corwyn, 2002). Scholars define socio-economic status to include "social capital" as resources (e.g., the number of parents one has at home, presence of a grandparent in the home). Other class status predictors include residential location, amount of consumption, and even types of recreational activities engaged in (Allen, 2004).

"Class" now has multiple, contested definitions. Stuber (2006) claims that class' meanings "must be understood as situated constructions that emerge organically, dynamically, and contextually" (p. 291). Subjective interpretations guide our perceptions of class status and thus negate an objective definition of class. For example, two students with similar financial income could have different class identifications, citing family background, occupation, and other cultural differences as reasons. One or both of these students could identify with multiple class categories and thus make class boundaries subjective.

Despite the pervasiveness of class difference and the universality of class experience, scholars frequently ignore class because it connects to other aspects of identity such as race, age, gender, and sexuality. Class is so intersected with other aspects of identity that it becomes hard to isolate or singularly define. Researchers sometimes disagree how social class' definition and how it affects identity, but they agree that it impacts people's lives (Allen, 2004; hooks, 2000; Moon, 2001).

Class often impacts classroom success (Lehmann, 2007; Oldfield, 2007; Priebe, Ross, & Low, 2008; Snell, 2008). Walpole (2003) found that students from lower socio-economic backgrounds generally "work more, study less, are less involved, and report lower GPAs" than their middle-class peers (p. 63). Similarly, lower- or working-class students often experience concerns about social mobility (Saldana, 1994; Walpole). FGS often worry about economic capital (i.e., the ability to find and maintain financial aid for tuition, housing, and additional resources) and cultural capital (i.e., parent's educational and occupational level, knowledge, and skill sets). Consequently, Lehmann argues that "non-traditional university students—whether first-generation, working class, or low income students—often encounter an acute sense of discontinuity between their social origins and their anticipated destination" (p. 96). Their language use, the inability to share experiences in the classroom, and lack of knowledge of campus resources are obstacles as FGS become aware of their class position within the higher education context.

Class Consciousness

As government funding makes the university accessible to diverse student populations, more students experience dissonance between their class background and campus culture. Students may develop class consciousness, or awareness of class differences, based on class markers such as regionality, language use, conversation topics, and personal appearance. In a 2009 study on college students who identify as lower- or working-class, Lawless found that many of these students do not realize their belonging in class categories until they transition into a university environment. Respondents made statements such as, "I used to think I was middle class until I was applying for college. When I was filling out the FAFSA I just looked up the poverty line and I was shocked. I couldn't believe that we were actually in poverty and didn't know it," and "I know one thing: when I moved to college, it was the first time I really felt like being poor was a bad thing. I loved the way I grew up and I wouldn't change it for the world, but college just made me more cynical" (p. 38). These experiences demonstrate the uncertainty and awkwardness that can exist for lower-class students entering college.

In addition to income class markers, some lower-class American dialects insert an "r" (making words such as "wash" sound like "warsh"), utilize non-standard English slang, or draw out vowel sounds. Regional language characteristics identify a person's neighborhood, knowledge of diversity, and even ethnicity, which are components of cultural capital that signify class position. Bernstein's (1960) classic work on language and social class highlighted the importance of these differences when he wrote, "Linguistic differences, other than dialect, occur in the normal social environment and status groups may be distinguished by their forms of speech. This difference is most marked where the gap between the socio-economic levels is very great" (p. 271). What is considered casual conversation for lower- and working-class students tends to be a clear class marker when put into an unfamiliar class context.

Topical conversation is a central part of cultural differences between home and campus. Engen (2004), Moon (2001), and hooks (2000) describe how conversations with friends and family changed after entering college. When FGS learn the rules of higher education they start to use academic jargon, think more critically about themselves and their position in society, and discuss previously undiscussed topics. It becomes difficult for FGS to code switch when returning to the once familiar home context. Hence, FGS face the dual identity crisis of not belonging in the academy or home.

Classism

FGS often experience cultural and emotional alienation due to classism, which is defined as prejudice or discrimination against individuals with lower-class status (Martin, 2008). Langhout, Rosselli, and Feinstein (2007) list six different types of classism, including: stereotype citation, institutionalized classism, interpersonal classism via separation, interpersonal classism via devaluation, interpersonal classism via discounting, and interpersonal classism via exclusion. Each type of classism carries distinct actions and behaviors.

"Stereotype citation" is classism reflected in stereotypic stories about lower- and working-class individuals. For example, instructors use stereotype citation if they state that all lower- or working-class students have poor literacy rates. "Institutionalized classism" occurs when organizational rules or structures create privilege some individuals. This type of classism might include not being able to take classes because of additional fees or not joining student organizations because the hours conflict with a work schedule. "Interpersonal classism via separation" occurs when an individual is separated from others in order to "protect" that person from being confronted by a higher class. Separating persons because of assumed class backgrounds perpetuates divisions between classes. Divisions like this might appear in exclusive fraternities and sororities or types of on-campus housing where having money affords students more opportunity.

"Interpersonal classism via devaluation" occurs when hostile or rude behavior targets someone who identifies as lower or working class. Devaluation explicitly marginalizes persons based on their experiences. "Interpersonal classism via discounting" goes a step further than devaluation by dismissing the burdens of the lower and working class. Examples of classism via discounting might include encouraging students to buy books and other resources they cannot afford or being dismissive of their financial concerns.

Finally, "interpersonal classism via exclusion" takes the form of "behaviors directed at a person that are perceived as excluding that individual from an event or activity because of his or her lower social class status" (Langhout, Rosselli, & Feinstein, 2007, p. 150). This type of classism could include a teacher inviting students to an exclusive paid event to see a guest speaker. Langhout et al. found that each of the six classism types are frequently used inside the college context both institutionally and from individual instructors.

A common act of classism occurs when an individual makes assumptions about another person's class background. In their qualitative study of first-generation college women from the working class, Wentworth and Peterson (2001) isolated the unfounded expectation that working-class students are motivated by money or social mobility (p. 18). The respondents claimed they were frustrated by interactions with college educated people and often felt inadequate when peers made assumptions about their financial, collegiate, or familial goals. Wentworth and Peterson describe the discontinuity between a pre-college identity and a current or post-college identity, its connection to socio-economic status, and the tension and alienation these women feel in college.

In light of the cultural transitions FGS experience, administrators, staff, instructors, and other students must be aware how social class impacts students' identities and college experiences. Faculty are all-too-often unaware of how their actions affect others. Like any other identity category, class status implies norms regarding appearance, activities, or even beliefs and values. Take, for example, the American Dream. Many Americans believe that upward mobility is possible through hard work and determination. For the middle class, it is not so much a dream because it is attainable and often achieved. For lower- and working-class citizens, this normalized goal may never be actualized. Yeskel (2008) describes the "centrality of public schools and public higher education to attaining the American Dream," pointing out this concept's reinforcement through various socialization tools (p. 1). When staff and faculty promote the American Dream and social mobility, they assert naturalized class ideals such as professionalism, non-colloquial language, and personal achievement.

When teachers unconsciously take certain beliefs and values for granted, they implicitly question the value systems of "the other" and hold their values at a higher worth. For example, college is often assumed to be training for professional careers. Although many FGS value professionalism, this is certainly not the only factor motivating them to obtain a degree. Making this false assumption erases other reasons for continuing education, such as gaining general knowledge or becoming the first family member to go to college. Some people are proud of their working-class background and it is an injustice to assume that everyone strives to be middle or upper class. Many college teachers who enact classism are unaware about how their actions can marginalize FGS. Thus, we must examine pragmatic approaches for avoiding classism.

A Pragmatic Approach to Classism in Your Classroom

Research on FGS describes literacy, integration, and retention as indicators of academic success (Horwedel, 2008; McKay & Esrella, 2008; Vohra-Gupta, 2007). I will now offer specific ways to avoid classism in the classroom and thus ensure FGS success.

First, do not make assumptions. Stereotyping occurs because class is often an invisible identity category. Lott (2002) relates classism to stereotypes and negative assumptions by explaining how our perceptions may cause us to separate, exclude, and discount individuals we think are of the lower or working class. Not all FGS are from the lower or working class. Moreover, we cannot assume that we understand a person's entire identity based on a few (if any) experiences that they share in class. Making assumptions about who is upper class or lower class perpetuates the problem of marginalization and erases personal experience. Instead of stereotyping, create a safe place for students to share their own experiences. Palmer (1993) describes this space as a mutual place of "truth telling" where room is created "not to make learning painless but to make the painful things possible, things without which no learning can occur—things like exposing ignorance, testing tentative hypotheses, challenging false or partial information, and mutual criticism of thought" (p. 74). Assumptions and stereotypes are avoided when the teacher and students learn from each other.

Not every classroom allows students to share experiences during class time, for a lecture hall with one hundred students may not be ideal for individual sharing. However, instructors can creatively find other opportunities to create intellectual space. For instance, a teacher can encourage students to share experiences through writing assignments or during office hours. In addition, teaching assistants can be trained to be cognizant of class issues and create a comfortable atmosphere for students from all class backgrounds.

Centralize class issues in your classroom. Even though many instructors now address race, gender, and sexuality, class is often still left out. Gardner, Dean, and McKaig's (1989) auto-ethnographic account recounts their experiences with the lack of openness about class. Dean writes, "It was within a traditional course on introductory sociology that I first heard my class background discussed. In that class, 'the working-class experience' was presented as an object to be studied, rather than as a possible experiential reality for students in the room. I felt not only invisible but dehumanized" (p. 68). The amount of class research pales in comparison to publications on other identity categories. We need to create more dialogue about class experiences as a part of human identity. Critical pedagogy creates a space where first-generation college students can explore the intersection of class with other aspects of identity.

In order to avoid these types of stories, there are concrete ways that instructors can increase dialogue about class and encourage their colleagues to do the same. If race, sexuality, ethnicity, or other identity components emerge in classroom discussion, challenge students to think about class. Devote equal discussion time to social class. For example, set aside a day to talk about class. I assign academic articles that analyze class and its intersection with other identity aspects. By giving your students opportunities to examine race or gender through a class lens, you create space for complex experiences to unfold and give students strong examples of how different pieces of identity intersect. Find class-related books, movies, or other resources in your institution's library and encourage your institution to purchase them if there are few or no resources. Finally, by having conversations about class-sensitive pedagogical ideas with your colleagues, class will become central in educational dialogue.

Be an ally to students. McKay and Estrella (2008) suggest that "interaction with faculty appears to be a significant factor in realizing academic and social integration for first-generation college students" and "quality of interaction with faculty is related to first-generation students' perceptions that they will accomplish short and long term academic goals" (p. 367). Provide support and validation to FGS. In their comparison study of traditional continuation college students and nontraditional FGS, Terenzini et. al. (1994) found that their instructor support made them feel capable of learning and instilled a sense of "obligation to succeed" (p. 67). The student respondents identified several characteristics of a validating instructor that included: positive communication, which instills a sense of belonging;

class activities structured to include their class experiences; and time, energy, and interest noticeably invested into the students.

Furthermore, be a faculty resource if you have a lower-class or FGS background. Because being from a lower- or working-class background is devalued, FGS frequently find it hard to share their struggles with others. Students need support from other people in their position, especially if that person has a position of power. In my teaching, I create an activity that enables students to share their experiences by literally stepping out in front of their classmates and identifying the different parts of their identities that are marginalized. I always participate and step out with the other "lower-class" students who identify with statements like, "I struggled to find funding for college" or "My family is currently or has been on some form of government assistance." Each classroom is different and the environment has to be one of respect and comfort for activities like this, but I encourage you to create ways to show your identity to the class.

If you consider yourself to be from a higher class, be aware of how you look, speak, and act in the classroom. It may be challenging to break away from the social parameters of what a teacher should look and act like, depending on your institution. However, awareness of how we represent our class is an important step for making FGS comfortable in their new environment.

Conclusion
Every classroom has a different dynamic and each student brings a different experience to the table. As educators, recognizing that FGS brings a unique yet underrepresented perspective into academia is imperative for creating a space that is respectful and appreciative of all. It is hard to recover from being told that you "don't fit in" or "you lack the skills necessary to succeed in college." Though some students who experience such classism are resilient, they should not have to be. Instead of creating more stories like mine, educators should create new stories of truth, strength, valor and most importantly, success for FGS.

References
Allen, B. (2004). *Difference matters*. Long Grove: Waveland Press.
Bradley, R. H., & Corwyn, R. F. (2002). Socioeconomic status and child development. *Annual Review of Psychology, 53,* 371-99.

Bernstein, B. (1960). Language and social class. *The British Journal of Sociology, 11(3)*, 271-276.

Cabrera, N. L. (2004). Entering and succeeding in the 'culture of college': The story of two Mexican heritage students. *Hispanic Journal of Behavioral Sciences, 26*, 152-170.

Engen, D. (2004). Invisible identities: Notes on class and race. In A. Gonzalez, M. Houston, & V. Chen (Eds.), *Our voices: Essays in culture, ethnicity, and communication* (4th ed.). (pp. 250-255). Los Angeles: Roxbury.

Fussell, P. (1983). *Class.* New York: Ballantine Books.

Gardner, S., Dean, C., & McKaig, D. (1989). Responding to differences in the classroom: The politics of knowledge, class, and sexuality. *Sociology of Education, 62(1)*, 64-74.

hooks, b. (2000). *Where we stand: Class matters.* New York: Routledge.

Horwedel, D. M. (2008). Putting first-generation students first. *Diverse: Issues in Higher Education, 25*, 10-12.

Langhout, D., Rosselli, F., & Feinstein, J. (2007). Assessing classism in academic settings. *The Review of Higher Education, 30*, 145-184.

Lawless, B. J. (2009). *Moving up in class? A study on college students' transition to academia.* Unpublished masters thesis, San Francisco State University, CA.

Lee, B., & Paek H. (2005). Values, cultures, and stereotypes of the professional middle class portrayed in the white palace. *Conference Paper – International Communication Association*, 1-23.

Lehmann, W. (2007). "I just didn't feel like I fit in": The role of habitus in university drop-out decisions. *Canadian Journal of Higher Education, 37*, 89-110.

Lott, B. (2002). Cognitive and behavioral distancing from the poor. *American Psychologist, 57*, 100-110.

Martin, J. (2008). Pedagogy of the alienated: Can Frierian teaching reach working-class students? *Equity and Excellence in Education, 41*, 31-44.

McKay, V. C., & Estrella, J. (2008). First-generation student success: The role of faculty interaction in service learning courses. *Communication Education, 57*, 356-372.

Moon, D. (2001). Interclass travel, cultural adaptation, and 'passing' as a disjunctive inter/cultural practice. In M. J. Collier (Ed.), *Constituting cultural difference through discourse* (pp. 215-240). Thousand Oaks: Sage.

National Center for Educational Statistics. (2005). *First-generation students in postsecondary education: A look at their college transcripts.* Re-

trieved from http://nces.ed.gov/pubsearch pubsinfo.asp?pubid
=2005171

Oldfield, K. (2007). Humble and hopeful: Welcoming first-generation poor and working-class students to college. *About Campus, 11,* 2-12.

Palmer, P. (1993). *To know as we are known: Education as a spiritual journey.* San Francisco: Harper.

Priebe, L. C., Ross, T. L., & Low, K. W. (2008). Exploring the role of distance education in fostering equitable university access for first-generation students: A phenomenological survey. *International Review of Research in Open and Distance Learning, 9,* 1-12.

Saldana, D. H. (1994). Acculturative stress: Minority status and distress. *Hispanic Journal of Behavioral Sciences, 16(2),* 116-128.

Snell, T. P. (2008). First-generation students, social class, and literacy. *Acadme, 94,* 28-31.

Stuber, J. M. (2006). Talk of class: The discursive repertoires of white working- and upper-middle-class college students. *Journal of Contemporary Ethnography, 35,* 285-318.

Terenzini, P. T., et. al. (1994). The transition to college: Diverse students, diverse stories. *Research in Higher Education, 35(1),* 57-73.

Vohra-Gupta, S. (2007). First-generation college students: Motivation, integration, and academic achievement. *Community College Journal of Research and Practice, 31,* 963-975.

Walpole, M. (2003). Socioeconomic status and college: How SES affects college experiences and outcomes. *The Review of Higher Education, 27(1),* 45-73.

Wentworth, P. A., & Peterson, B. E. (2001). Crossing the line: Case studies of identity development in first-generation college women. *Journal of Adult Development, 8(1),* 9-21.

Wong(Lau), K. (2004). Working through identity: Understanding class in the context of race, ethnicity, and gender. In A. Gonzalez, Houston, M., & Chen, V. (Eds.), *Our voices: Essays in culture, ethnicity, and communication* (4th ed.). (pp. 256-263). Los Angeles: Roxbury.

Yeskel, F. (2008). Coming to class: Looking at education through the lens of class. *Equity and Excellence in Education, 41,* 1-11.

CHAPTER THREE

UNTIL MR. RIGHT COMES ALONG: SOCIAL MOBILITY, HIGHER EDUCATION, AND THE LURE OF CULTURAL ELITISM

JoAnne M. Podis

During the past ten years or so, I've had essentially the same conversation with several beginning instructors from varying disciplines and, thankfully, follow-up meetings that suggest those discussions have been helpful as they solidify their teaching philosophies. The salient issue in these talks has been the instructors' lack of consideration of contextual influences, particularly with respect to class, on both their students and on themselves. For the most part these inexperienced young professors come from households more privileged than those of their students, and they have found unexpected difficulties in teaching students with working-class backgrounds.

From their points of view, such students have been quick to challenge their authority; they didn't seem to understand higher education protocols that they, the professors, took for granted; these students were very job-oriented, valuing education solely as a means to an end—employment. They pushed back immediately when the instructors tried to assert themselves in terms of rigid rules and regulations, the only strategy anyone else had ever mentioned to them as fledging teachers ("Be firm; don't let your students take advantage of you!").

All of these newly minted assistant professors also believed in education as the path to social mobility, and they believed as well that their students could learn—so why weren't their students responding to them in the ways they had hoped? They wound up approaching me, whom they viewed as an experienced, and, I assume, effective, classroom teacher, for advice.

As we began discussing the issues, I suggested in each case that perhaps in their efforts to claim their own authority, they were coming across as disrespectful and heavy-handed, and that perhaps students were seeing them as links in the chain of The Man—that it was not about standards, but about fair application of standards, and that if they could see students' questions or challenges as their efforts to make sense of a totally unfamiliar culture, they might then view the students differently.

Rather than squelching questions, they might just go ahead and answer them, for example, and not take them as personal affronts to their status in the classroom. They might consider more carefully the context in which they were teaching and, especially, the personal contexts within which their students operated, since most were so very different from the instructors' own backgrounds and experiences. They might stop expecting them to know how to negotiate the academy's demands and try rather to help them do so, all the while also helping them to reach the learning goals of the course.

Firm in their own good intentions, these young professors had genuinely never considered that respect might be an issue for their students. Once they did so, their relationship with their students began to improve, and their heightened awareness of social and class differences began to work in their favor. For example, one instructor had instituted a "zero-tolerance" attendance policy with respect to absences. She was somewhat stunned to find that some of her students did not have reliable transportation (our campus is not served well by public transportation and is completely inaccessible via that mode on weekends). The first time a student presented her with "my car died" as a reason for missing class, she dismissed it out of hand as an excuse, not a reason, and refused to allow the student to make up the work. Once she had rejected the first request for an excused absence, she felt she would lose face if she reconsidered when subsequently more than one student ran afoul of her policy. She quickly gained the reputation of being cold and unfeeling, and her relationship with the class began to suffer as a result.

The students felt disrespected because in their minds they had valid reasons for missing class (not always transportation-related, as child care is an issue for many of our students as well). The next semester the instructor stressed the importance of class attendance but also allowed for excused absences. She had taken for granted that students had the wherewithal to attend and assumed that they would be scamming her if they claimed they lacked what in her mind was something that "everyone" has. Her policy was based on the assumption that students had backgrounds similar to her own; when she attended college, she had no responsibilities other than studying, and transportation was not an issue because she lived on campus.

Many years before, I had been in some ways in the same position. I too was a brand-new assistant professor with limited teaching experience—white, female, and very, very young. I also had some notions, which I will share below, that would have predicted a far different response many years later to my young colleagues' requests for guidance in teaching their classes.

My background was solidly working class. My mother, a Bohemian immigrant who came to this country in her early twenties, worked as a housekeeper for a wealthy family for fifty years; my father, likewise a Bohemian immigrant, was a carpenter, as was his father before him. Like many immigrants, my parents, in particular my mother, had drummed it into me that education was my way out of the working class and into a middle-class, white-collar lifestyle. Langston (1993) in her essay "Who Am I Now: The Politics of Class Identity," notes that, although their mother lacked knowledge of college protocols, she seemed to "live vicariously through the possibility" (p. 62) of her daughter's earning a degree. My mother seemed to do the same.

All this parental attention had a distinctly gendered spin. From my mother, I heard the phrase "to fall back on" inextricably and always linked to any phrase like "a career" or "a job." Equally intimately linked were "as a teacher" or "as a nurse"—the whole package thus became, "a career/job as a teacher/nurse to fall back on." My professional ambitions were thus confined to two scenarios: first, I would be able to support myself during the process, assumed to be relatively brief, of finding a husband. Second, in the event of the unfortunate and presumably precipitous demise of said husband, I would have a means of support to which to return. I've learned that my experience is an echo of countless others—Annas (1993) in "Pass the Cake: The Politics of Gender, Class, and Text in the Academic Workplace," notes that the same relentless expression, to "fall back on" (1993, p. 167) was prominent in her upbringing, and Langston (1993, p. 63) stresses her family's focus on good marriages for their daughters.

I dutifully responded to my mother's insistence on education as the key to success by applying myself to my studies and receiving acceptance to the most selective private university in the region. My parents were thrilled, within the parameters given above. (Is all this the reason I did my dissertation on Jane Austen, I sometimes wonder—this relentless focus on marriage and family?)

I excelled as an undergraduate and had no difficulty receiving acceptance to graduate school. It should be noted here that I did not tell my parents about my plans to do graduate work, since there is no way that I would have been encouraged to delay (even potentially) marriage and family. Covertly I obtained enough financial assistance for advanced study without asking them for support and proceeded with my plans. As I pursued my degrees (enough to boil water, as a friend used to say, lest I become too full of myself), I was quickly seduced by the lure of becoming a professor—professing my pearls of wisdom to small numbers of student-acolytes and publishing esoteric articles that would rock the scholarly world. At the same time I would acquire the trappings, the *things* that would represent integration into middle-class America, the same impulse Sennett and Cobb identified in their classic text *The Hidden Injuries of Class* (1973, p. 18). I would have a spacious office and bookshelves lined with books that I owned—not borrowed from the library. I might occasionally bring my purebred dog to the office with me. I would live in a large home in a leafy suburb close to campus where my neighbors would be fellow faculty members. And I would travel to professional conferences in exotic locations—exotic being pretty much anywhere outside my home state, as travel had been something my family could not afford.

Thinking back to my college career, I realize that I always felt somewhat on the margins, although pledging a sorority in my sophomore year made me feel more a part of campus culture, as did moving on campus senior year. My friends at the university tended to be those with whom I was most comfortable—commuters rather than residential students, working-class rather than middle or upper, a small group that stuck together in the student union.

Except when I was with this small circle, I concealed my background as much as I could (and I'm not proud of this, by the way). No surprise there: "Universities are designed to make working-class people feel like we don't belong. Because we don't" (Kadi, 1993, p. 92). I found myself constantly trying to "pass" for middle-class, which created a good deal of stress as I struggled to be sure to keep up the front and not let the façade slip with an incautious comment or action that might reveal my background.

In the event, as I completed my graduate work expecting to be scooped up by a Research I where I would receive a starting salary that would enable my move up the social ladder, I learned to my chagrin that somehow jobs—jobs with benefits, jobs anywhere—had become very scarce indeed. Adding a preferred location to the scenario reduced one's chances even further and resulted in my exceedingly quick acceptance of an offer—from, horror of horrors, a *business college* that had in the fairly recent past been a proprietary institution. Offering me a position was part of the college's strategy to improve its image in higher education by hiring doctorally-prepared faculty. My dissertation director, demonstrating her complete ignorance of anything so practical as making a living (she was decidedly *not* of the working class), said something like, "Well, you're not going to take *that* job, are you?" Indeed, I was, and I did.

Instead of teaching literature, I found myself teaching mainly first-year composition and business writing and research at what could be described as the sort of "third-rate university" at which Peckham suggests working-class academics often wind up (1995, p. 274). Nevertheless, it was an exciting time in that writing pedagogy was undergoing a complete transformation. Further, since I was at a small college that prided itself on a learning/student focus, I was able to apply the new pedagogy in my classrooms. Instead of teaching grammar independently and out of context, I began to use examples from the students' papers to illustrate grammatical principles. I worked one-on-one with students on their drafts, and I also used peer-editing workshops to provide as much feedback as possible to students, and to provide them with a sense of themselves as writers writing to an audience of more than just the instructor. In short, I did all the things that have now become standard-issue in composition courses.

In accepting a position at a college only marginally above open admission, and in my hiring's being considered part of the institution's strategy to raise its status and lift its profile in the higher education community, I now understand that I did not face many of the well-documented barriers that working-class women in the academy have encountered and continue to face. I proceeded through the rank and tenure process with nary a ripple; so far as I ever knew, my salary was commensurate with the position and comparable to those of men at the institution. It probably helped that the female administrator who hired me was a formidable presence at the college, and thanks to a highly regarded secretarial program, about half of the faculty were female.

I also didn't have to worry about another issue—students making snide remarks about my class background. They were themselves primarily working-class, many of them also sons and daughters of European immigrants. Others were students of color, and many were poor, receiving the maximum college, state, and federal assistance and having to work full-time besides. Like me, they viewed education as the way out—out of the inner city, out of minimum wage jobs, and into the middle-class mainstream. Education meant earning "certificates for social mobility and job choice" (Sennett & Cobb, 1973, p. 24). Unlike me, though, they came to college in many cases ill prepared to do the work required, and this was especially true of the younger students. Their high school educations had been abysmal, and their writing skills were basic at best, their interest in reading or writing non-existent. They were sold on the value of a college degree but did not possess the skills necessary to obtain one. The college had begun a federally funded student support services program in response, but these students generally needed a lot of personal attention and a lot of one-on-one work with their writing. My teaching situation could not have been more different from what I had expected it to be.

It was under these circumstances that I discovered that social justice, one of the values most dear to me, kicked in, big-time. I saw in these students what I might have been—if I had been black rather than white, if I had gone to weaker public schools, if I hadn't aced every standardized test I ever met, if, if, if. I too had held minimum-wage jobs to support my education and had punched a time clock (vowing the while never to do so again). And I felt that I could help my students improve their lives—an attitude altruistic, idealistic, impractical—maybe all of these, but heartfelt as well.

I tried to create learning environments that were respectful and collaborative. I worked with students to create learning outcomes and establish standards for their writing. In responding to what students wrote, I tried to make my assessments as supportive as possible within the parameters that grading of necessity entails. I also offered students the option of creating their own assignments if none of the prompts I created captured their fancy. I encouraged open discussion. I tried to guide those discussions gently, without stifling debate but rather enabling it, even if students made inappropriate or incorrect statements. At those times, I asked follow-up questions intended to elicit further explanations or clarifications, or provided some additional information and asked the student to consider further what she had said.

I pictured myself in those students' places and how I would appreciate being treated. I tried at all times to behave justly within an unequal power relationship and have been rewarded and privileged on many occasions to be witness to "the transformation" of working-class women (La Paglia, 1995, p.183) who have returned to higher education after a gap of many years. My students have consistently praised the respectful and open atmosphere in my classrooms over a career that now spans three decades. "She wants us to learn," "She is caring and nurturing and makes all class members feel important," and "She is kind and cares about her students," are representative comments, and the words "fair" and "respectful" are probably the two terms that pop up most frequently in my evaluations.

I am not suggesting that having a working-class background is the only route to a democratic educational philosophy; I know, though, that in my own case, it did have an influence in moving me away from a high-culture, elitist perspective into a more egalitarian one.

In my current teaching setting, at a liberal arts college more selective than the institution at which I began my career, my classroom is filled with students of all kinds—multi-generational, multi-racial, multi-class—and I enjoy the diversity. I teach mainly seniors and often have second-degree students, which is of course a very different audience from the basic skills students I used to teach, and the content differs as well. The senior-level course is a literature course, not a writing course, thus there is a much lower volume of paper grading to be done, and even more emphasis on discussion, which, as I say above, I have always emphasized in preference to lecture.

In most ways, it's a much easier sort of teaching I do nowadays—have I indeed achieved the practical equivalent of my graduate student dreams, I wonder—but my commitment to democratic classrooms remains and always will be a basic tenet of my educational philosophy. The senior seminar I teach is based on the novels of Jane Austen and the film versions thereof, a rich field in which to mine both class and gender consciousness, and I do so with gusto. Many of my students seem vaguely surprised to have their beliefs in the classlessness of U.S. society challenged—do I engage them in such discussions at least in part because of my background? I suspect I do. Thankfully, I am at a women-focused college where women's issues are always on the table, and where the creation of a just society is integral to college mission, so I don't need to explain why both tend to take a prominent place in our discussions of texts.

Throughout my career, and even despite my current access to privileges that would startle my parents, my working-class background has had a positive influence. My parents may not have expected me even to have my own career, let alone to hold a senior management position, but they certainly taught me to value the transformative power of education, to *work hard, and to take pride* in whatever work I did, principles that have played a huge role in whatever success I have achieved. When I work with students from similar class backgrounds, it is easy for me to recognize in them the same passion to better themselves and to succeed against the odds. Over the years I have moved from first denying then obscuring my background ultimately to reclaiming from it what was positive.

Having made this journey is, I suspect, what enables me to advise effectively instructors who come from more privileged circumstances and who may misread as inappropriate challenges to their authority the responses of working class students for whom "the best defense is a good offense." Simply asking them to interrogate the assumptions they make about their students and their students' abilities to negotiate the academy and then to identify how those assumptions may diverge from their students' realities can be a critical first step in becoming a more effective instructor. Standards are absolutely necessary for quality, but standards leavened with a little empathy ensure that all are treated justly and respectfully.

References

Annas, P. (1993). The politics of gender, class and text in the academic workplace. In Tokarczyk, M., & Fay, E. (Eds.), *Working-class women in the academy: Laborers in the knowledge factory* (165-178). Amherst: University of Massachusetts Press.

Dews, C. L., & Law, C. L. (Eds.) (1995). *This fine place so far from home.* Philadelphia: Temple University Press.

Gardner, S. (1993). What's a nice working-class girl like you doing in a place like this? In Tokarczyk, M., & Fay, E. (Eds.), *Working-class women in the academy: Laborers in the knowledge factory* (49-59). Amherst: Universityof Massachusetts Press.

Kadi, J. (1993). A question of belonging. In Tokarczyk, M., & Fay, E. (Eds.), *Working-class women in the academy: Laborers in the knowledge factory* (87-98). Amherst: University of Massachusetts Press.

La Paglia, N. (1995). Working-class women as academics: Seeing in two Directions. In Dews, C.L., & Law, C.L. (Eds.), *This fine place so far from home* (177-186). Philadelphia: Temple University Press.

Langston, D. (1993). Who am I now? The politics of class identity. In Tokarczyk, M., & Fay, E. (Eds.), *Working-class women in the academy: Laborers in the knowledge factory* (60-72). Amherst: University of Massachusetts Press.

Miner, V. (1993). Writing and teaching with class. In Tokarczyk, M., & Fay, E. (Eds.), *Working-class women in the academy: Laborers in the knowledge factory* (73-86). Amherst: University of Massachusetts Press.

Peckham, I. (1995). Complicity in class codes: The exclusionary function of education. In Dews, C.L., & Law, C.L. (Eds.), *This fine place so far from home* (263-276). Philadelphia: Temple University Press.

Ryan, J., & Sackrey, C. (1996). *Strangers in paradise: Academics from the working class*. Lanham, MD: University Press of American, Inc.

Sennett, R., & Cobb, J. (1973) *The Hidden Injuries of Class*. NY: Vintage Books.

Tokarczyk, M., & Fay, E. (1993). (Eds.) *Working-class women in the academy: Laborers in the knowledge factory*. Amherst: University of Massachusetts Press.

MEETING THE CHALLENGES OF FIRST-GENERATION STUDENTS THROUGH ACADEMIC PROGRAMS

◆ CHAPTER FOUR ◆
THE ROLE OF GENERATIONAL STATUS, PROGRAM AFFILIATION, AND CULTURAL BACKGROUND IN THE PERFORMANCE OF COLLEGE STUDENTS

Alice Araujo and Andreas Anastasiou

First-generation college students are alternately defined as those whose parents' highest educational level is a high school diploma or lower (Upcraft et al., 2006; Giancola, Munz, & Trares 2008); and as those whose parents have not attended a postsecondary institution (Wang & Castaneda-Sound, 2008; Hand & Payne, 2008).

First-generation college student status is seen as adversely affecting academic performance, motivation, persistence, and graduation. Although more likely to take a lighter course load than fellow students whose parents hold a four-year college degree (Pike & Kuh, 2005), first generation college students tend to earn lower grades (Pascarella et al., 2004). On the other hand, this student population has been found to have an internal locus of control (Hand & Payne, 2008), suggesting that a sense of self-efficacy can play a key role in first-generation college students' sense of their own chances for academic success.

Nonetheless, parents' lack of experience with college tends to adversely affect their children's success in transitioning from high school to college as well as their post-secondary experience such that FGS are less likely to graduate from college than their continuing-generation counterparts. Poor academic preparation, lower educational aspirations, reduced encouragement and support from families, limited knowledge of the college application process, limited financial resources to afford college, and adjustment issues regarding the academic, social, and cultural norms of academic culture all adversely affect the experience of this group (Engle et al., 2006).

Such variations in "cultural capital" based on parents' educational background have been linked to differences between traditional and first-generation college students' mastery of the student role and ability to meet faculty expectations (Collier & Morgan, 2008). Unlike their continuing-generation counterparts, first-generation college students cannot rely on the motivating influence and experience of their parents for knowledge and support regarding decisions about college. Such experience was found to contribute to a better preparation for the culture of higher education (Pearson et al., 2008; Pascarella et al., 2004).

The differences in the college experience of this group have led some researchers to regard first-generation college students as a special population with unique needs and challenges (Lippincott & German, 2007; in Wang & Castaneda-Sound, 2008), "often overlooked, marginalized," and "at risk" in terms of academic success (Hand & Payne, 2008), persistence, and graduation (Kuh, 2008 in "It's all"). Indeed, Pike and Kuh (2005) found first-generation college students to be less likely to form relationships with other students and members of the faculty. Relationships and emotional support, both formal and informal, have been identified as playing a major role in students' persistence in college through their greater academic and social integration within an institution (Tinto, 1993; Harrell & Forney, 2003; Pascarella & Chapman, 1983; Terenzi, 1980, in Hand & Payne, 2008).

Satisfaction with campus life has also been found to be diminished by a student's first-generation status, perhaps due to their limited involvement in campus life and longer work hours off campus relative to their continuing-generation counterparts (Pike & Kuh, 2005). Not surprisingly, first-generation college students are more likely to come from a low-income family background, and to therefore experience financial stress (Hand & Payne, 2008; Upcraft et al., 2006).

Students report their first-generation college status as particularly salient to their identities at the outset of their university careers and post-graduation (Orbe, 2004). This more vulnerable group of students often act as family "delegates" by fulfilling their parents' dreams of college (London, 1989; in Hand & Payne, 2008). In a study of first-generation college Appalachian students, Hand and Payne (2008) found that this group experienced the not uncommon university student conflict between independence and loyalty between home and family most acutely, although most felt supported by their parents and were expected to attend college.

The unique challenges posed by a first generation college status have in fact been regarded as akin to bouncing between the two often contradictory cultures of home and academia (Hsiao, 1992, in Wang & Castaneda-Sound, 2008). The successful negotiation of these identity tensions plays a key role in academic success (Orbe, 2008). It is with the role of two variables that might influence academic success in college—i.e. students' generational status and cultural background—that this study concerns itself.

Purpose

The purpose of this study was to investigate the effects of program affiliation and cultural background on academic success (as reflected by GPA) of first-generation and continuing-generation college students. First-generation college students (defined in this study as those whose parents never attended college) are compared to continuing-generation college students (i.e. those whose parents did attend college). Based on the existing literature on the subject, we predicted that first-generation college students will demonstrate significantly lower grade point averages (GPAs) in college relative to their continuing-generation counterparts.

Operational Definitions of Variables

Program affiliation: Students' membership in the institution's various programs targeting different age groups and specific interests. In this study, the programs included consisted of: the residential program for exceptionally gifted students as young as rising 8th-graders and with an average age of 14; and the military leadership program for students interested in public service careers with a focus on the military.

Generational status: "First-generation" was defined as students whose parents never attended college.

Success: Students' grade point average (GPA) in college was used as the measure of success.

Cultural Background: A student's self-identified cultural identity as belonging to a white (majority) group or to a member of a minority group.

Method

Participants

Data from participants forming the undergraduate student body of a private four-year all-women's liberal arts college in the mid-Atlantic region was utilized as the basis for this study.

These data were collected by the College's institutional research team and was made available to the authors for the purposes of this study.

Demographic characteristics

The sample group was comprised of the 568 undergraduate women in the residential college, which includes the traditional program, the program for the exceptionally gifted, and the military leadership program. Of these, 366 were white students and 132 were minority students or students of color. First-generation whites comprised 124 students in the sample, while first-generation minority students made up 55 students of that sample. Continuing-generation whites formed 242 students in the sample, whereas 77 students were included in the continuing-generation minority students of the sample. The approximate ages of the students in the traditional program and in the military leadership program ranged between 17-22. The age of the exceptionally gifted students ranged between 13 and 16.

Results

Analysis of the data using independent samples T-tests supported the hypothesis that first-generation college students would demonstrate significantly lower success in college as reflected by their grade point averages (GPAs). In addition, this investigation further examined the role of generational status in several other subgroups. More specifically, we compared first-generation and continuing-generation students' performance by program affiliation and by cultural background. Table 1 shows comparisons by program affiliation while Table 2 displays comparisons by students' cultural background based on their self-identification as members of a minority or majority (white) group.

White students' GPAs were significantly higher even when first-generation white students' GPAs were compared with those of first-generation minority students. This seems to suggest that cultural background could be a moderating variable.

There were no significant differences on the basis of program affiliation alone with the exception of the academic performance of students in the program for exceptionally gifted students. There were also no significant differences between continuing-generation students in the traditional program and continuing-generation students in the military program. However, a most interesting and unexpected finding was that, contrary to our hypothesis, there were no significant differences between first-generation minority and continuing-generation minority students.

Discussion

The data in this study strongly suggest the key role of both generational status and cultural background in college students' performance regardless of program affiliation. Students whose parents attended college overwhelmingly fare better than those of parents who did not. This is consistent with the findings of Pascarella et al. (2004). We also found that first-generation white students have lower GPAs than their continuing-generation counterparts.

When compared on the basis of cultural background, however, white students fared consistently better, regardless of generational status. As such, continuing-generation whites performed better than continuing-generation minority students. It is noteworthy, however, that *first*-generation white students also performed better than did continuing-generation minority students whom the literature suggests that, on the basis of generational status alone, would benefit from the parents' experience in college (Collier & Morgan, 2008).

Similarly and perhaps most significantly, continuing-generation minority students did not significantly differ in their scores from their first-generation counterparts. These findings strongly suggest a significant role of cultural background in predicting academic performance among FGS that could be explained by other factor(s) such as socioeconomic status (SES).

There could be a link between cultural background and SES making the latter a better predictor of academic performance. This connection is consistent with the findings of Hand and Payne (2008) that low-income students are more likely to experience stress that could adversely affect their academic performance. Engen (2004) points out that working class individuals' view of class discussions and education itself as essentially functional means to an end—"to get things done" and to secure a good job and a good life, respectively--often clashes with the more traditional educational approach that places a premium on education as a means to understand the self as well as to develop one's thinking and creative self.

Also, working class students' forms of expression often clash with those valued in higher education so that those students experience their new academic environment as a new culture that utilizes and values different forms of communication and espouses a different worldview regarding education. The ensuing communicative struggles serve to alienate students of lower socio-economic backgrounds. Unfortunately, this current investigation did not include SES data. Therefore, it is suggested that any future study includes SES as an important demographic variable. In Orbe's (2008) research, identity markers like race, socioeconomic status, and age—and their interplay—serve a central function in FGS' sense of self and negotiation of their various cultural identities.

This study also suggests that program affiliation does not play a role in students' academic performance, not surprisingly with the exception of the program for the exceptionally gifted. According to the most recent data available at the time of publication, students in that program entered the College with an average SAT score of 1790 (based on a three-score rating) and an average GPA of 3.84. Consistently with the main findings of this study, all exceptionally gifted program students in the sample had parents who had attended college, again pointing to the importance of generational status in students' successful performance.

Another interesting finding was that the performance of first-generation residential students was significantly higher than that of first-generation military students.

One possibility for these results could be the fact that typically, students from the latter program come from lower SES. The literature indeed links lower SES to greater levels of stress (Hand & Payne, 2008; Upcraft et al., 2006). In addition, this physically and mentally demanding program design significantly increases the level of stress that participating students experience, in preparation for military careers.

The College's continuing efforts to promote the enrollment, retention, education, and graduation of first-generation college students through a variety of academic and social initiatives include a hands-on, instructional admissions and enrollment approach involving students and their families, learning communities, paired courses, student mentors, intensive programming for high-risk students, and placing first-year students in a section of their academic advisor for closer monitoring. Extensive programming for minority students has also greatly expanded since the opening of an office of African American and multicultural affairs in the mid-1990's that emphasizes personal mentoring and the cultivation of pride in students' cultural identities. In addition, retention strategies have been implemented in the institution through an emphasis on individual attention reflected in an average class size of 16.7 and a student/faculty ratio of 10:1.

In spite of these comprehensive initiatives and strong support system, the data in the study suggest that such efforts have not gained enough traction with FGS, a group that the literature suggests faces greater challenges than their continuing-generation counterparts by being much more vulnerable to the multiple pressures of financial stress, job demands, academic preparation, homesickness, and other personal issues (Collier & Morgan, 2008; Engle et al., 2006; Pascarella et al., 2004).

Recommendations for Future Studies
The results of this case study must be reproduced in a comparative study of different institutional types to also include coed, medium and large size institutions, as well as research and technical educational institutions. In addition, this study did not examine age as a variable in the experience of FGS. Such data would be essential for education institutions to provide greater support for students in adult degree program students.

Because much of the literature varies in their definitions of first-generation college student status, a comparative study of mothers and fathers and their varying individual educational experience (e.g. having attended college or not, having graduated college or not), might yield interesting data about the relative role of each parent in the support of the experience of their children in college as well as the relative role of different levels of parental educational status. The role of socioeconomic background must also be examined for a more nuanced understanding of the role cultural background plays in the experience of first-generation college students.

Finally, qualitative data derived from focus groups and in-depth interviews with first-generation and continuing-generation students, as well as with minority and majority students, would more comprehensively assess the experiences of these groups of students from their perspective. Rich, in-depth data from the perspective of students themselves would provide needed insight into their experience and negotiation of the "third space" or "third culture" of students'

FGS status in contrast to those of majority students. Such studies would offer greater explanatory power of the results of this study.

A more comprehensive understanding of the role different variables affect FGS of multiple identities will provide needed data to better assist colleges and universities most effectively implement institutional efforts that preemptively address the experience and needs of students of less traditional backgrounds.

Limitations

This study did not include age, gender, or different institutional types as additional variables for consideration. In additional, the single-institution sample limits the comparative value of the data, although findings were consistent with much of the literature on the subject.

Most importantly, perhaps, the research did not include SES as a demographic variable. In light of our results here, this may be the most relevant variable that begs further examination in future studies.

References

Carnevale, A. P., & Fry, R. A. (2000). *Crossing the great divide: Can we achieve equity when Generation Y goes to college?* Princeton: Educational Testing Service.

Collier, P. J., & Morgan, D. L. (2008). "Is that paper really due today?" : Differences in first-generation and traditional college students' understandings of faculty expectations. *Higher Education*, 55, 425-446.

Engen, D. (2004, 4th ed.). Invisible identities: Notes on class and race. In A. Gonzalez, M. Houston, & Chen, V. (Eds.), *Our Voices: Essays in culture, ethnicity, and communication* (pp. 250-255). Los Angeles, CA: Roxbury Publishing Company.

Engle, J., Bermeo, A., & O'Brien, C. (2006). *Straight from the source: What works for first-generation college students.* Washington, D.C.: Pell Institute for the Study of Opportunity in Higher Education.

Giancola, J. K., Munz, D. C., & Trares, S. (2008). First- versus continuing-generation adult students on college perceptions: Are differences actually because of demographic variance? *Adult Education Quarterly* 58 (3), 214-228.

Hand, C., & Payne, E. M. (2008). First-generation college students: A study of Appalachian student success. *Journal of Developmental Education* 32 (1), 4-15.

It's all about execution (2008). *Newswire*, 22 (7), 6-7.

Nunez, A. M., & Cuccaro-Alamin, S. (1998). *First-generation students: undergraduates whose parents never enrolled in postsecondary education.* Washington, D.C.: U.S. Department of Education, National Center for Education Statistics.

Orbe, M. P. (2004). Negotiating multiple identities within multiple frames: An analysis of first-generation college students. *Communication Education*, 75, 249-284.

Orbe, M. P. (2008). Theorizing multidimensional identity negotiation: Reflections on the lived experiences of first-generation college students. In Azmitia, M., Syed, M., & Radmacher, K. (Eds.). *The intersections of personal and social identities. New Directions for Child and Adolescent Development*, 120, 81-95.

Pascarella, E. T., Pierson, C. T., Wolniak, G. C., & Terenzini, P. T. (2004). First-generation college students: Additional evidence on college experiences and outcomes. *The Journal of Higher Education*, 75, 249-284.

Pearson, J. C., Carmon, A. F., Child, J. T., & Semlak, J. L. (2008). Why the range in grades? An attempt to explain the variance in students' public speaking grades. *Communication Quarterly*, 56 (4), 392-406.

Pike, G. R., & Kuh, G. D. (2005). First- and second-generation college students: A comparison of their engagement and intellectual development. *The Journal of Higher Education*, 76, 276-300.

Snell, T. P. (2008). First-generation students, social class, and literacy. *Academe* 94 (4), 28-31.

Trenor, J. M., Yu, S. L., Waight, C. L., & Sha, T. L. (2008). *Journal of Engineering Education* , 449-465.

Upcraft, M. L., Gardner, J. N., & Barefoot, B. O. (2006). *Challenging and supporting the first-year student: A handbook for improving the first year of college.* San Francisco, CA : Jossey-Bass.

Wang, C-C. D. C., & Castaneda-Sound, C. (2008). The role of generational status, self-esteem, academic self-efficacy, and perceived social support in college students' psychological well-being. *Journal of College Counseling*, 11, 101-118.

Table 1
Comparisons by Program Affiliation

Groups Compared	N	Mean GPA	P-Value
1st-Generation Traditional	164	2.74	
Continuing-Gen. Traditional	289	2.95	<.05*
1st-Generation Traditional	164	2.74	
1st-Generation Military	41	2.55	<.05*
1st-Generation Traditional	164	2.74	
Continuing-Generation Military	52	2.96	<.05*
Continuing-Generation Traditional	289	2.95	
1st-Generation Military	44	2.51	<.05*
Continuing-Generation Traditional	289	2.95	
Continuing-Generation Military	52	2.96	>.05
Continuing-Generation Gifted	20	3.33	
1st-Generation Military	44	2.51	<.05*
Continuing-Generation Gifted	20	3.33	
Continuing-Generation Military	52	2.96	<.05*
Continuing-Generation Gifted	20	3.33	
1st-Generation Traditional	164	2.74	<.05*
Continuing-Generation Gifted	20	3.33	
Continuing-Generation Traditional	289	2.95	<.05*
ALL Continuing-Gen. Students	359	2.98	
ALL 1st-Generation Students	209	2.69	<.05*

* Asterisk denotes statistical significance

Table 2
Comparisons by Cultural Background

Groups Compared	N	Mean GPA	P-Value
1st-Generation Whites	124	2.85	
Continuing-Generation Whites	242	3.14	<.05*
1st-Generation Whites	124	2.85	
1st-Generation Minorities	55	2.45	<.05*
Continuing-Generation Whites	242	3.14	
1st-Generation Minority Students	55	2.45	<.05*
1st-Generation Whites	124	2.85	
Continuing-Generation Minorities	77	2.52	<.05*
Continuing-Generation Whites	242	3.14	
Continuing-Generation Minorities	77	2.52	<.05*
1st-Generation Minorities	55	2.45	
Continuing-Generation Minorities	77	2.52	>.05

* Asterisk denotes statistical significance

◆ CHAPTER FIVE ◆
HUMBLE AND HOPEFUL: WELCOMING FIRST-GENERATION POOR AND WORKING CLASS STUDENTS TO COLLEGE

Kenneth Oldfield

Students who are the first in their family to enter higher education join a rarified and often mystifying culture of rules, rites, and rituals.

A first-generation working-class college student who became a faculty member offers his insights and recommendations after forty years in the academy.

While sexism, racism, homophobia, and other prejudices offend most Americans, both inside and outside the academy, fewer people articulate the profound effects of social-class bias. For example, professors seldom detail the considerable advantages that the offspring of parents who hold college or university degrees possess. Admittedly, some faculty discuss social class in the abstract, but rarely do they describe how socioeconomic forces shape their own campus and their own life or depict the benefits that parents with college educations from the middle or top socioeconomic classes bequeath to their children.

Because of my humble background, I experienced my socioeconomic status (SES) as a lack of cultural capital as I headed off to college. Cultural capital is the knowledge, skills, education, and other advantages a person has that make the educational system a comfortable, familiar environment in which he or she can succeed easily. Cultural capital is what I did not have. My parents and grandparents never finished high school. They all worked blue-collar jobs ranging from truck driver to restaurant cook to janitor. I had mediocre college entrance examination scores and average high school grades. I still marvel at how little I understood about the higher-social-class sensibilities of university life when I started college.

It was only much later and through my own reading and personal conversations with other first-generation working-class college students that I came to understand why high-SES values predominate at college. It is mostly a case of majority rule, given that college students and professors are disproportionately from high-SES backgrounds. In *Equity and Excellence in American Higher Education*, William Bowen, Martin Kurzweil, and Eugene Tobin (2005) report that poor and working-class students are significantly underrepresented at nineteen of the nation's most selective universities. Only 11 percent of students at these schools were from families in the lowest income quartile, whereas 50 percent were from families in the highest income quartile. Anthony Carnevale and Stephen Rose (2003) reported similar findings in their study of 146 of the nation's most prestigious colleges and universities. These researchers and others note the strong connection between socioeconomic origins and academic achievement. Pierre Bourdieu (1986) explains that even when low-SES students are qualified for admission to highly selective schools, they often lack the cultural capital necessary to apply.

In response to the noted underrepresentation of poor and working-class students at selective institutions, Bowen (2005) and his colleagues as well as Carnevale and Rose (2003) recommend that these institutions begin to recruit more applicants from disadvantaged origins who have promising entrance scores. Bowen and his colleagues suggest that once leading institutions start recruiting more applicants from among low-SES students, colleges and universities everywhere will follow suit. While I applaud these egalitarian recommendations, I also know firsthand that there is far more to expanding learning opportunities than simply enrolling a more socioeconomically diverse student body. First-generation college students from poor and working-class backgrounds must understand that their new surroundings will require much more from them than just getting good marks. No matter what distance they have physically traveled to their campus, college requires a cultural journey to a very different land than the one they knew as youngsters. For first-generation poor and working-class college students, surviving the social challenges of higher learning can be at least as demanding as achieving a high grade point average.

To increase the odds that first-generation students with low-SES backgrounds will persist and prosper in college, it is vital that their chosen schools offer them an adequate social support system throughout their stay. These students must be helped to understand that they are entering a foreign culture, a place that can be quite forbidding. The problem is not that they cannot do the work; rather, it is their estrangement in their new surroundings. At college, they will meet people from families with advantages they can hardly imagine, including overseas travel, large in-home libraries, subscriptions to news and cultural magazines, the latest computer technologies, horse stables, chandeliers in the dining room, luxury cars, fine clothing, and so on. This description applies not just to the nation's leading institutions but to many other schools, though perhaps to a slightly lesser degree.

Today, after spending nearly forty years in higher education, first as a student and then as a professor, I think more and more about how much easier college would have been had I known at the start what most of my privileged cohorts took for granted. Happily, direct experience is not the only teacher. Tales told by former poor and working-class first-generation college students can help today's newcomers survive and prosper in the academy. For one, these accounts can encourage other students and help them see that they are not the first to feel alone and intimidated in the land of higher education. Second, such stories can help poor and working-class first-generation college students recognize that they can surmount the challenges they face, especially if they avail themselves of services designed to smooth their path.

Personal narratives can also help faculty and administrators see why it is necessary to change the campus environment so that first-generation college students with humble economic backgrounds feel more at home there. Likewise, making the campus more inviting can enrich the lives of students and professors of more privileged origins. Democratizing higher education so that it represents a more complex reality and more diversity in terms of SES will help privileged groups gain a greater respect and appreciation for the values and survival skills their fellow travelers bring to campus. With proper nurturing, certain so-called disadvantages can be reinterpreted as differences rather than shortcomings. In sum, the ultimate goal should be reforming the campus culture so that it better reflects the lives of all who go there, irrespective of their socioeconomic background.

Finally, the comments in the following section are not meant as an end in themselves; rather, they are meant as a foundation. I will conclude the commentary by proposing four reforms that all colleges should enact: first, institutions need to ensure that their first-generation poor and working-class college students are being properly oriented to college life, and second, they need to change their campus environment so that all students gain a deeper appreciation for how SES and social-class origins affect the trajectory of all our lives.

Six Lessons That I Wish I Had
Known Before Going to College

Lesson 1: I wish I had known the difference between a "doctor" and a "doctor." I had never heard of a Ph.D. until I encountered higher education. At West Liberty State College, my undergraduate school, most professors held master's degrees, but a few had Ph.D.'s. Two of my first-semester teachers introduced themselves as "doctor." I was confused but too scared to ask for clarification. Later in that first week, as I was walking by various faculty offices, I noticed that some had "Dr." on the door nameplate. Seeing some of these titles, I wondered why this college would hire physicians to teach subjects such as speech, German, and history. It made some sense that M.D.'s would teach the natural sciences, but not business or the humanities; why would someone with all that earning power take a relatively low-paying job? Perhaps they did the work on the side? That seemed unlikely. Even after learning the difference between a Ph.D. and an M.D., it was hard to see the former as real doctors, like those who order lab tests, prescribe medicines, do surgery, or pull teeth.

Later, as a Ph.D. student, I discovered another twist on the "real doctor" versus "not a real doctor" theme. I had become friends with several medical students, and they sometimes kidded me about not being a real doctor. I consulted a dictionary and learned that *doctor* comes from Latin and means "to teach." After that, anytime my medical school friends ribbed me about not being a real doctor, I would explain this etymology and say, good-naturedly, of course, that unless they went into teaching they would not be real doctors. I was a doctoral student before I finally learned the original intent of the degree I was seeking.

My initial lack of understanding about these terms was symptomatic of my status as an academic outsider. Research indicates that my peers whose parents had higher socioeconomic status would have developed a significantly larger vocabulary and better language skills early in life. In addition, they would have received more reinforcement for scholastic achievement. Thus, they would likely have heard their parents use the word *doctor* to refer to professors as well as physicians or to describe career options.

Lesson 2: I wish I had known the real purpose of college before I started. I was far along in my studies before I finally learned why most middle and upper-class families insist that their kids attend a college or university. I had assumed that a college's only purpose was job training. While I enjoyed reading Ibsen's plays and learning about the discovery of DNA, I kept wondering how this was making me more employable. Meanwhile, my non-college-going, working-class high school chums were building strong earning skills in practical fields such as barbering, jet engine repair, and telephone installation.

One day, another student recommended a certain course to me, saying the teacher was especially good. My friend was right, and then some. The instructor, a man of conspicuously privileged origins, was enthralling from the start. Besides lecturing, at each meeting, he encouraged us to discuss our views about that day's topic. I quickly understood his teaching strategy. He wanted everyone to value doubt and curiosity. The only proposition he rejected outright was an unwillingness to wonder and challenge, even if it meant disagreeing with him. He never lowered your grade if your views differed from his.

One afternoon, maybe halfway through the term, the class was debating some point about formal learning and a student began arguing that higher education should be reformed to make it "more relevant." He wanted college to give people more "job skills, and not all this literature and philosophy stuff." I was thinking, "My thoughts exactly!" The professor paused for a moment and then explained, "No, the primary purpose of an undergraduate degree is to teach you more ways to enjoy life. Studying literature, politics, science, art, theater, and philosophy should prepare you for a richer existence, not employment. Go to a trade school if you only want job skills."

There it was: the kind of wisdom that distinguishes great instructors from the rest. This professor's words washed over me in revelation. How I wish I had known that secret all along. When you grow up hearing family members and neighbors rightly saying that they are lucky to have work, it is hard to think that anyone would spend money on something as ethereal as ensuring that their children have a more enjoyable life rather than a better job.

Since that distant afternoon, I have never heard a better rationale for a liberal arts education. In only a few sentences, this professor had given me an insight that most of my privileged friends treated as a birthright. I finally saw why they valued knowledge for its own sake. As children, they had learned to see the world as a welcoming place where they could expect to succeed. In such a world, higher education served not as an opportunity to better one's economic chances but rather as a socially accepted way to explore new interests.

Ever since that day, it has seemed ironic to me that those who could most benefit from college—as measured by the value that would be added to their lives—are least likely to attend. Even if everyone from the poor and working classes took the same job they would have had without an undergraduate degree, they would still gain the most from a college education because it would teach them more ways to escape the humdrum existence of everyday employment—knowledge that all should receive, not just those raised in privileged circumstances.

Lesson 3: *I wish I had known that teeth are such a strong social-class marker.* My mother and my grandparents had lost all their teeth early, and my mother always blamed everyone's dental problems on their having "weak teeth." If you had "strong teeth," they pretty much lasted whether you cared for them or not. If you had "weak teeth," no matter how often you brushed, they still decayed and had to be extracted. Brushing after every meal was unheard of in my house. As a youngster, I went days without brushing my teeth. My parents never once insisted that I brush my teeth.

I remember my surprise when I started grade school and saw that every one of the teachers still had most if not all of their natural teeth. Granted, they had fillings or sometimes badly stained teeth, but at least they were real teeth, not the perfect kind that I associated with dentures.

By the time I was ten years old, five of my permanent teeth were so rotten that oral surgeons had to remove them. When I started college, all of my teeth had been filled at least once. Based on what I had learned at home, I assumed that nearly everybody over the age of forty wore dentures, and I was well on my way to that fate.

In college, the relationship between dental health and social-class origins was even more obvious. From the first day, I marveled that so many faculty and students had "strong teeth." Because many of my professors were over forty, I expected that most would wear dentures. I do not recall any who did.

The dental story continued in graduate school. Although most of the school janitors, cafeteria cooks, and maintenance workers had missing teeth or dentures, few of the other M.A. and Ph.D. students or the faculty had visible fillings, and none had false teeth. Some even had "movie star teeth." Among students and faculty, having "strong teeth" seemed as common as having attended strong elementary and secondary schools. Apparently, the same subtle advantages that provided access to schools with well-paid teachers and superior physical facilities also resulted in mouths with real, dazzling white, and perfectly straight teeth.

After I became a professor, I overheard some colleagues talking about *Nell*, the movie starring Jodie Foster, so I watched it. It was about a twenty-something woman who was a "wild child," much like the lead character in François Truffaut's film of that name. Nell lived alone in a cabin in very rural North Carolina and, evidently, spent her entire life beyond the benefits of civilization. When Nell first appears partway through the movie and opens her mouth in a close up, you see that she has movie star teeth. Despite a lifetime living away from modern amenities, Nell has radiant white teeth and no conspicuous dental problems. Laughable! Maybe she just had "strong teeth." Talk about a movie blooper! It was like seeing a computer sitting on a rock in the movie *One Million Years B.C.* In all my college days, no professor, not even any of the self-proclaimed Marxists, ever mentioned the relationship between social-class origins and dental health. Maybe it was because they all had "strong teeth." But when you grow up seeing so many people with "weak teeth," you notice these things.

Lesson 4: I wish I had known that college is not just for "smart people." As a youngster, I had assumed that a degree was well beyond my capabilities. I knew that if I went to college, I would flunk out in the first semester. After all, nobody in my family or neighborhood had finished college, so what were my chances? Moreover, between back surgery and flunking first grade, I started college two years behind my high school cohorts. This gave many of them sufficient lead time to quit or flunk out of college before I even started. This group included a woman who had ranked in the top twenty of our class. These facts, combined with my mediocre high school grades, made me believe that my days in higher education would be numbered. Unlike my peers from high-SES backgrounds, I had gained neither the social nor the intellectual skills necessary for academic and professional success. So like many students from poor and working-class families who fear academic failure, I spent most of my first semester wondering where I would be working come January after receiving my first-term grades.

I had rarely studied in high school, other than a short while the night before a test. I took these study habits to college. Not surprisingly, I did not do well during the early part of my first term, and because my parents had never attended college, I couldn't ask them for advice on how to do better. I had to figure it out on my own. Near the end of the semester, I tried studying several days before each test. I started getting A's and B's. Still, I feared that I had found religion too late for salvation.

Because my college, like most others, only distributed report cards after each term, I had no idea what grades to expect. I still assumed that I would flunk out. My academic survival hinged on the salvage work that I had done in the last part of that first term. I was astonished when I opened my grades that cold January morning. I did not get my report card until I went to school for second-term registration, meaning that if I had flunked out, the news would have traveled quickly because I would have not been allowed to register. I would have had to leave the building and walk past all the students standing outdoors in line, waiting to enroll. My first-term grades were two B's and three C's—to me, the equivalent of being on the "Nobel Prize Honor Roll." Although I did not know it then, my newfound study habits would help me make the dean's list every semester after my first year. I barely missed making the list in the second term of my first year. My GPA was 3.22, just 0.03 below the threshold. In my graduate school classes, I got one B and the rest were A's.

I eventually learned that my undergraduate grades shocked others as well. In my junior year, a friend said that a relative of his (whom I will call Tom)—the son of a wealthy family in my hometown—had flunked out of college and was moving home. After helping him return his belongings to his room, his mother sat on the side of his bed and began crying. Tom asked her what was wrong, and she sobbed, "Oh Tom, I just don't understand. If Ken Oldfield can get through college, anyone can. What's wrong with you?!" Tom had been socialized in the ways necessary to succeed in college at all levels, both socially and academically. He, like his peers raised by well-educated and high-earning parents, was statistically more likely than I was to complete advanced and professional degrees. But Tom never did finish college. First-generation poor and working-class college students who laugh last . . .

Lesson 5: I wish I had known that higher education considers debate and argument integral to sound learning. In my hometown, when two working-class kids disagreed about something important, they began by speaking louder and louder until one of them backed down. If the matter remained unsettled (meaning that the physically weaker one had not relented), they started fist fighting. After settling the matter, they usually went several months before talking to each other again. Sometimes this silence lasted a lifetime.

In college, everything was upside down, for faculty and students alike. I was shocked to learn that you were *expected* to question other students, in class and out. In the best courses, the professors encouraged you to debate *them*.

During one of my first days on campus, I was sitting at a table in the student union beside two professors and some students. They were all hotly contesting some point. The students appeared to me to be juniors and seniors, and they were just as likely to disagree with one or both professors as they were with each other. I do not recall what they were debating, but I expected to see them fist fighting any second.

I left for class, and when I returned an hour later, I was amazed to see the same people still sitting at the table, warmly chatting about something altogether different, as if there had never been any disagreements. Obviously, there were no hard feelings. I later realized that if anything, these disputes make the contestants better friends. It is still hard for me to accept that sometimes students or faculty pick arguments just to test an idea.

Obviously, no college is free of backbiting and alienation, but first-generation poor- and working-class college students should know beforehand that colleges and universities view disagreement as fundamental to quality learning. Exchanging loud words is not the last stage before a fistfight, as I always thought.

Lesson 6: I wish I had understood how the academy defines work. Until college, I never realized how much my social-class origins affected how I interpreted the word *work*. During my first few weeks on campus, I was amazed to see people who could earn a good living doing what professors do, especially given that they never produced anything practical such as haircuts, cars, or toasters. Moreover, all the professors wore formal clothing while on campus. They never went home smelling of work, as my family always did. Faculty could go straight from campus to a fancy restaurant and fit right in. I found this new culture—in which a day's work remained, in large part, invisible—alienating and even intimidating.

Not only did professors not have real bosses who watched over them, but they did not have to work summers and holidays. As a first-year student, I heard someone say that every so many years, professors could take off one semester at full pay. They called it a *sabbatical*, which the dictionary said is Hebrew for "rest." When I read this, I thought, "Rest!? From what!?" After several semesters, I started thinking, "Maybe I should see about getting into this line of 'work.'"

Even today, when I hear students or professors claim they are working, I am tempted to say, "You wanna see work!? I'll show you work! I'll take you to the greasy spoon my mother and grandmother *worked* in for at least eight hours a day, six days a week, flipping burgers and making French fries while standing on a cement floor. During summers, the kitchen temperature often exceeded 100 degrees. *That's* work!" The academy taught me why it is called "the working class."

Finally, I deciphered that faculty say that working-class people have "jobs" but middle- and upper-class folks have "professions." When I first noticed this distinction, I consulted a dictionary and found that *amateur* comes from the Latin word *amare*, meaning "to love." An amateur does something for fun, such as playing a pickup game of basketball for grins. The dictionary also said that *professional* means paying people for what they do. Loretta Lynn (1976) should have called her autobiography *Professional Coal Miner's Daughter.*

In "The Quest for Equity: 'Class' (Socioeconomic Status) in American Higher Education," Bowen (2004) offers an especially telling summary of the relationship between SES origins and education. He writes," It is the long-term, lasting effects of SES on both cognitive and non-cognitive skills (including motivation, attitudes, social skills, and 'proper' behavior) that . . . are the main determinants of differences in educational opportunity. Put another way, poor families have great difficulty investing sufficient resources to develop in their children in the time before high school graduation, the abilities and outlooks necessary to enable their children to attend college and graduate" (pp. 8–9). In short, just by being the son or daughter of high-SES parents, a child gains far more of the social and cultural capital needed to perform better in formal education at all levels.

Four Suggested Reforms

Nothing in the preceding paragraphs is meant to disparage anyone in my family or the neighbors that I knew as I was growing up. By definition, none of the people from back then had the privilege of being privileged. They did the best they could with what they had.

That said, I will use the preceding section as a foundation for the four reforms I propose that all institutions adopt to better meet the unique needs of their first-generation poor and working-class students. These reforms are double-edged. On one hand, they involve ways to help students with humble beginnings adjust to and succeed in their new circumstances. On the other hand, they suggest ways to reform the campus learning environment so that it reflects a more diverse socioeconomic reality. The latter changes will help students of high-SES origins gain new insights into social-class matters that differ considerably from the ones they are currently leaving campuses with. At present, colleges and universities mostly reinforce assumptions that privileged individuals bring to higher learning. Thus, the reforms I am suggesting can enhance learning for all students.

Reform 1: Develop support systems for poor and working-class first-generation college students. Most colleges and universities have specialty student organizations or research centers to address the needs of particular groups (for example, women, students of color, or GLBTQ students). Institutions should establish comparable facilities to meet the unique needs of poor and working-class individuals. These centers should help students acquire important cultural capital by showing them how to obtain financial assistance, how to locate and use campus resources, how to minimize costs (for example, by buying used instead of new textbooks or laptop computers), and how to secure reasonable housing. Center directors should organize special orientation meetings for all interested first-generation college students in order to address major challenges that newcomers face, such as selecting appropriate courses, developing effective study habits, taking tests, and writing term papers.

Each first-generation college student should be provided with both a peer and a faculty mentor, preferably ones who are or were first-generation college students themselves. These mentors would help orient their student to the college experience and support the student's transition in the first year. In turn, as sophomores, first-generation college students should be encouraged to be peer mentors for new incoming students. Special center advisors could handle issues unique to the junior and senior years, such as questions about résumé writing, standardized test preparation courses, and graduate and professional school admissions. Mentors and center advisors could identify students who need additional assistance. In the end, these centers would be money-saving ventures. By reducing the first-generation college student dropout rate by just a few percentage points, these facilities will pay for themselves. Providing these support systems is a productive first step toward assisting first-generation college students. Another crucial task is altering the campus environment to address and reduce social class discrimination.

Reform 2: Address classism. The preceding recommendation suggests ways to help first-generation college students, particularly poor and working-class students, adjust to the culture of higher learning. It is equally important that we change the campus environment to be inclusive so that privileged students are encouraged to understand and appreciate the values reflected in poor and working-class students' ways of life. Faculty and administrators must encourage *all* students to become multicultural in regard to class issues.

One way of facilitating class multiculturalism is by having faculty members introduce social-class concerns into all their courses. Middle- and upper-class students must be exposed to materials that tell them more about poor and working-class people, promoting an understanding of the countless hurdles that students from these backgrounds face while in the academy. A small sampling of possible texts includes Sherry Lee Linkon's *Teaching Working Class*, C. L. Barney Dews and Carolyn Leste Law's *This Fine Place So Far from Home*, Betty Hart and Todd Risley's *Meaningful Differences in the Everyday Experience of Young American Children*, and Mike Rose's *The Mind at Work: Valuing the Intelligence of the American Worker*. The centers that I described earlier could maintain databases of resources for faculty and student use.

Faculty should not confine their socioeconomic instructional efforts to studying the generic consequences of class. Students should be encouraged to research how SES plays out on their campus. They might, for example, compare the social-class origins of (1) fraternity and sorority members versus nonmembers; (2) professors versus campus service workers (for example, janitors, cafeteria cooks); or (3) in-state versus out of- state students. These hands-on studies could be especially effective in fostering students' appreciation of the long-term consequences of widely divergent socioeconomic backgrounds.

Finally, because professors are products of the system they are trying to transform, shifting the campus environment to include more social-class concerns will be as educational for many of them as it is for their students. Faculty members gain the highest return on investment when their intellectual travels take them far beyond their comfort zone, something the recommended reforms would surely do. Addressing classism requires changing faculty perspectives; it also requires changing the makeup of the faculty.

Reform 3: Diversify the social-class origins of the faculty. Bringing more diverse faculty perspectives to a campus enhances its learning environment. A similar rationale has been used to justify changing the race and gender composition of the faculty of an institution. Schools should expand their job notices to include wording that encourages persons from poor and working-class origins to apply. A background questionnaire that surveys socioeconomic origins should be included with all applications. All job applicants of humble origins should receive special attention in the selection process.

Nothing reconfigures the professoriate's assumptions about merit more than asking them to reinterpret the concept in a quest for greater faculty diversity. Paul Light (1994) shows in his article "'Not Like Us': Removing the Barriers to Recruiting Minority Faculty" that this new view of personnel selection need not come at the expense of quality. Considering social class in faculty hiring can reduce classist assumptions on the part of faculty and staff, bring diverse perspectives to campus, and support all students' success.

Reform 4: Diversify the social-class origins of the student body. A primary reason for recruiting more students of humble origins to enter higher education is to improve the learning environment by bringing a more diverse collection of opinions and experiences to campuses. All institutions should collect and maintain information on their students' socioeconomic backgrounds. Review committees should weigh information on social-class origin when deciding on admissions. Carnevale and Rose (2003) suggest that we view merit as a fluid concept: "While all striving has merit, striving against physical, social, economic, and cultural barriers is regarded as especially meritorious. In American culture, merit is measured not only by where one stands, but also by how far one had to go to get there. Americans are still willing to give special breaks to people who show 'the right stuff' in overcoming barriers" (p. 6). Considering social class in admissions could ensure a strong contingent of poor and working-class first-generation college students in the classroom, a critical mass that would help these students feel comfortable on campus and that would improve the quality of the learning environment for all students.

Conclusion

Collecting data on the socioeconomic origins of students and faculty would allow institutions to monitor the effectiveness of the proposed social-class-based diversity efforts. These data could help gauge retention rates, help staff and faculty understand the mix of SES backgrounds on each campus, help track academic majors and minors by SES origins, allow follow-up on students' application rates for graduate and professional schools, and aid in identifying grade point average problems among poor and working-class first-generation college students. In short, schools should use data on socioeconomic origin to assess which policies are most effective in addressing the needs of first-generation students from poor and working-class backgrounds. These data should prove especially helpful in identifying students who need individual interventions to facilitate their success.

One goal of these proposed campus reforms is to change the college environment to better reflect the needs and values of students who are first in their family to seek a college degree, especially those from humble economic backgrounds. An equally important goal is to strive for social equity by educating all students and faculty about social-class dynamics. Perhaps then the six lessons I wish I had learned before going to college would be easier for poor and working-class first-generation college students to learn, easing their cultural journey. If my professor is right that an undergraduate education is supposed to teach people how to lead richer lives, a significant part of this campaign should involve exposing all students to the hopes, values, and everyday realities of poor and working-class individuals. In this way, higher education can expand the social and intellectual horizons of *all* its participants.

References

Bourdieu, P. (1986). The forms of capital. In J. Richardson (ed.), *Handbook of theory and research for the sociology of education.* New York: Greenwood Press.

Bowen, W. G. (2004, April 7). Lecture II: The quest for equity: 'Class' (socioeconomic status) in American higher education. Paper presented at the Thomas Jefferson Foundation Distinguished Lecture Series, University of Virginia.

Bowen, W. G., Kurzweil, M. A., & Tobin, E. M., in collaboration with Pichler, Susanne C. (2005). *Equity and excellence in American higher education.* Charlottesville: University of Virginia Press.

Carnevale, A. P., & Rose, S. J. (March 2003). Socioeconomic status, race/ethnicity, and selective college admissions. New York: Century Foundation [http://www. tcf.org/Publications/Education/ carnevale_rose.pdf]. Retrieved Jan. 1, 2006.

Dews, C. L. B., & Law, C. L. (eds.). (1995). *This fine place so far from home: Voices of academics from the working class.* Philadelphia: Temple University Press.

Hart, B., & Risley, T. R. (1995). *Meaningful differences in the everyday experiences of young American children.* Baltimore: Paul H. Brookes.

Light, P. (1994). 'Not like us': Removing the barriers to recruiting minority faculty. *Journal of Policy Analysis and Management,* 13(1), 164–179.

Linkon, S. L. (ed.). (1999). *Teaching working class.* Amherst: University of Massachusetts Press.

Lynn, L., with Vecsey, G. (1976). *Coal miner's daughter.* Chicago: Regnery.

Rose, M. (2004). *The mind at work: Valuing the intelligence of the American worker.* New York: Viking.

Thanks to Elsie Bilderback and Madolyn Kimberly for helping with this project.

◆ CHAPTER SIX ◆
UNDERSTANDING THE IMPACTS OF SOCIOECONOMIC STATUS ON FIRST-GENERATION STUDENTS: A CASE STUDY

Harmony Paulsen and Jena Griswold

Introduction

The correlation between first-generation status and socioeconomic class has been repeatedly confirmed in national studies (Eitel & Martin, 2009; Pike & Kuh, 2005). A comprehensive study conducted Terenzini and associates in 1996 for the National Center on Postsecondary Teaching, Learning and Assessment indicated that first-generation students (FGS) tend to come from low-income homes. This finding was further supported by studies conducted by Inman and Mayes (1999) and Horn and Nunez (2000). FGS from low-income backgrounds are generally less prepared academically and are laden with non-academic demands that can impact academic and social acculturation to college. The experiences of FGS from low-income backgrounds differ appreciably from their non-first-generation peers prior to and during college largely because of socioeconomic background. In order to understand the experiences and address the needs of a sizeable segment of FGS at post-secondary institutions it is necessary to consider socioeconomic status.

This chapter focuses on the biggest factor that distinguishes the majority of FGS from their peers—socioeconomic class. Specifically, this chapter explores the institutional, social, and academic challenges faced by FGS at an existing small liberal arts college, herein referred to as SLA College. The majority of FGS at SLA College during this study self-identified as lower-middle or lower class, which is consistent with the findings of previous national studies. Each section of this chapter discusses the role of class in the college experiences of FGS. The sections conclude with a list of measures that can be implemented by college administrators, faculty and staff to support FGS from low-income backgrounds in achieving academic and social success. These recommendations were extracted from student suggestions included in the survey responses and interviews. While the measures recommended in this chapter are not comprehensive and may differ for each institution, they provide a starting point for colleges and universities to investigate and resolve institutional practices that may adversely impact FGS from low-income backgrounds.

Methodology

The objective of this study was to understand how the college experiences of FGS are influenced by socioeconomic background, particularly focusing on access to social and academic opportunities in college. Data was gathered through an electronic survey that was distributed to the entire student body via email and was made available on the Internet over the course of three months. The survey was conducted during the 2005-2006 academic year over a three-month period, during which time 474 of 1,492 students responded, representing a 32% response rate. The responses to all survey questions were sorted based on self-identification by socioeconomic category. The quantitative data in this study was supplemented by narratives taken from the open-ended questions from the survey.

Following the survey, 21 FGS were interviewed to add an additional narrative component to the study. Students were selected for an interview based on their involvement in an on-campus first-generation/working-class support and advocacy group. Ten of the 21 students self-identified as lower class, 7 self-identified as lower-middle class, and 4 self-identified as middle class. All interviewees were asked similar questions that were meant to expand upon findings from the survey.

Class Identity at SLA College

This section uses the results of the quantitative and qualitative surveys to define the demographic that is the focus of the chapter by describing the common trends identified amongst each class based on access to financial and cultural capital. This section demonstrates that FGS at SLA College typically hail from lower or lower-middle-class backgrounds and lays the foundation to further explore issues faced by FGS from low-income backgrounds.

All of the interviewees from the lower- and lower-middle-classes identified socioeconomic status as one of the most significant factors influencing their college experience. Sixty-six students (14% of survey respondents) were FGS. Of the FGS, 63% self-identified as lower- or lower-middle- class, while the remaining FGS largely self-identified as middle-class (29%). Lower-middle class and lower-class students comprise the majority of the first-generation demographic, with the percentage of FGS increasing in the lower classes. Of the students who self-identified as lower- and lower-middle-class students, 50% were first-generation as compared to 11% of the middle-class students and 3% of upper-middle and upper-class students (see Table 1). This study thus focuses on those students who self-identified as lower- or lower-middle-class (see Figure 1).

The results of the survey illustrated that SLA College students of the same socioeconomic class tended to share common characteristics. Individuals who self-identified as lower-class came from households with the lowest annual income (see Figure 2). Lower-class students were more likely to self-identify as an ethnic minority (see Figure 3). All lower-class students attended a public school in contrast to 48% of their upper-class peers and 20% of their middle-class peers who attended private or college preparatory schools. Lower-class students were more likely to work their way through school, and consistently worked more hours than their peers. The amount of parental education decreased incrementally by class, suggesting that access to resources in the home that facilitate college preparation was more limited for low-income students (see Figure 4).

Access to financial and cultural capital was a characteristic indicator of socioeconomic class. Access to capital in all forms can influence a student's sense of belonging, particularly if past experiences or access to material possessions determine their ability to meaningfully engage in social and academic activities to the same degree as their peers. Low-income students arrived at college with fewer material possessions (see Figure 5) and engaged in fewer cultural activities prior to college (see Figure 6).

Table 1. First-Generation Students

	Upper Class	Upper-Middle Class	Middle Class	Lower-Middle Class	Lower Class
Total # Respondents	24	194	171	56	28
# First-Generation Students	1	4	19	22	20
% First-Generation Students	4%	2%	11%	40%	71%

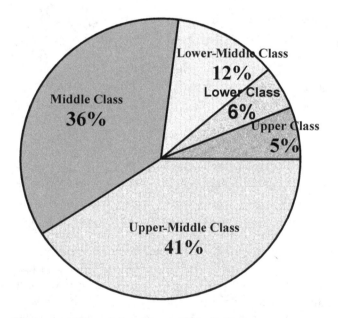

Figure 1. Class Identity at SLA College

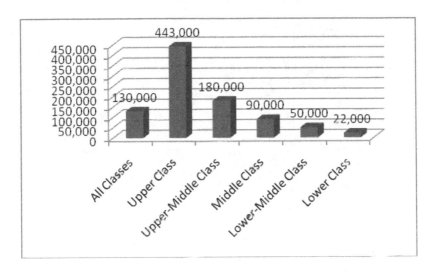

Figure 2. Average Family Income by Dollars

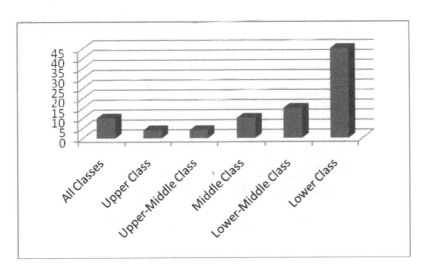

Figure 3. Ethnic or Racial Minorities

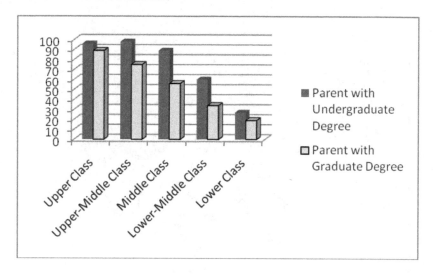

Figure 4. Parental Level of Education

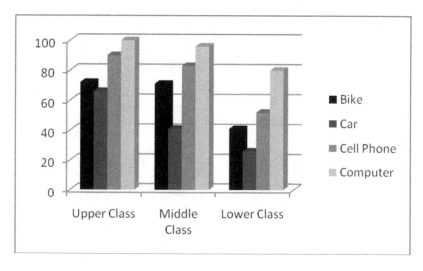

Figure 5. Material Possessions

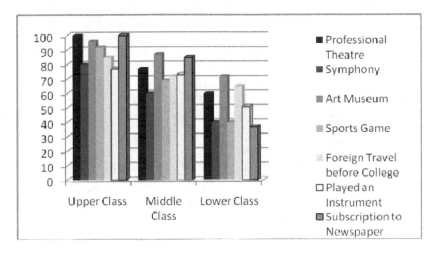

Figure 6. Pre-College Cultural Activities

While it is not the responsibility of college administrators to ensure that all students own the same material possessions or have the same pre-college experiences, administrators should be aware that access to financial and cultural capital may impact access to and success in other college activities. According to Eitel and Martin (2009) access to college does not translate into success. They found that first-generation female college students were not financially literate and this lack of literacy predicted their success or lack thereof in college experiences. This is an example of a concept that will be further explored in the following sections.

Institutional Environment
This section explores institutional challenges faced by FGS from low-income backgrounds and includes a list of recommendations provided by students to mitigate potential institutional disparities.

Class-based Discrimination
Low-income students cited an increase in class-based discrimination upon entering SLA college, while high-income students noted a decrease (see Figure 7). Middle-class students indicated that they did not feel more or less discriminated against at SLA College. All survey respondents were asked to describe any instances of discrimination that they experienced while at SLA College. Anecdotes provided in re-

sponse to that question are used to further elucidate the experiences and sentiments of low-income students in the following sections.

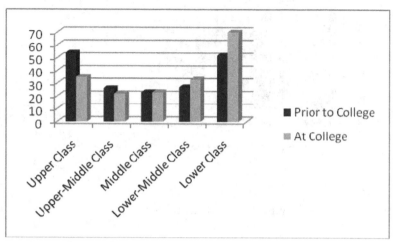

Figure 7. Experiences of Class-based Discrimination

Financial Aid

Many low-income students at SLA College were unfamiliar with the inner-workings of the college administrative system and expressed frustration when they attempted to navigate the system without a knowledgeable guide. Amongst the first-generation respondents, low-income students expressed more frustration given the greater degree of need and increased sense of financial vulnerability. Of the students that applied for financial aid, students from the middle or upper classes were 75% more likely to receive help from their parents in filling out financial aid forms or applying for both subsidized and unsubsidized loans (See Figure 8). Furthermore, financial aid calculations did not take into account that some parents cannot make parental contributions and that students may actually be making contributions to their family rather than the other way around.

Beyond issues of inadequate financial support, a number of first-generation, low-income students were unable to successfully communicate or negotiate their needs within the financial aid system. First-generation, low-income students struggling to maintain financial stability were intimidated by financial aid officers and felt discouraged from seeking additional financial aid, as illustrated by the following student's experience:

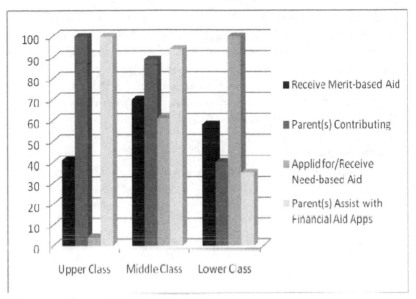

Figure 8. Financial Aid

I have felt discriminated against by the financial aid office. Since my freshman year my scholarship has been reduced by $6,000. When I asked the financial aid office about this they suggested I get another job on campus when I already had two jobs. They also said that my family should contribute more and I should be grateful for how much money they are giving me because "most kids leave here with $50,000 in loans." I guess they figure that most kids' parents make more than $27,000 a year too. They also probably figure that I'm not the one financially supporting my parents.

The FGS from low-income backgrounds were wary of their interactions with college administrators and were oftentimes embarrassed to explain their situations and ask for help. The observed hesitance by low-income students to seek assistance from college administrators is exacerbated by the fact that they are less likely to receive parental support or feel that they have an advocate at college.

Room and Board
At SLA College, freshman and sophomore students are required to live on-campus regardless of their finances, oftentimes paying more than twice what they would have to pay for off-campus housing. Furthermore, most residence halls require that students enroll in a

meal plan that charges $5 - $9 per meal. Low-income students on a tight budget struggled to pay thousands of dollars that they could have otherwise saved. Seven of the first-generation interviewees from low-income backgrounds petitioned to move off-campus during their sophomore year due to financial hardship; six of them were not granted permission to live off-campus or discontinue the meal plan based solely on financial considerations.

Recommendations

- Institutional Values/Admission Criteria: *Value employment to the same degree as extracurricular activities in the admission process. Value socioeconomic diversity to the same degree as multicultural diversity, particularly since they are oftentimes interrelated.*
- Financial Aid: *Create a welcoming environment in the financial aid office and help students understand all available resources. Create an emergency fund that students can apply to when faced with financial emergencies.*
- Parental Contributions: *Alter the calculation of financial need to account for the fact that some parents are unable to financially support their child and some children are financially supporting their families.*
- Room and Board: *Institutionally legitimate financial considerations when addressing room and board, namely the ability to live off-campus. Allow low-income students to remain on-campus during breaks if they do not have the resources to travel home.*

Social Environment

Social opportunities are an essential part of the college experience and allow students to pursue fulfilling activities beyond the classroom, oftentimes contributing significantly to a student's personal growth and future aspirations. Furthermore, social activities foster a student's sense of belonging or inclusion on-campus. Socioeconomic status can impact a FGS's integration with college culture and association with peers as discussed in this section.

Residence Life

In addition to overseeing on-campus housing for students, the Residence Life office seeks to create a sense of community through campus-wide events and residence hall activities. The freshman experience is significantly influenced by the social environment created in the dorms and the relationships fostered between section-mates.

While some residence-life events are free or subsidized, other events require money to participate. Low-income, FGS indicated that they felt estranged from their sections and dormitories when costs inhibited them from joining in the social camaraderie. One student explained his/her feeling of isolation:

> There are many people at [college] who were brought up [in] very comfortable, if not privileged economic situations. They often tend to assume that everyone that goes [to college here] is from a similar background, and sometimes just don't "get it" when money is an issue for me. Other students, especially in my section, often make hurtful comments about class situations, about clothing, about my inability to participate in activities. I don't think that they necessarily intend to be hurtful; they seem to be acting out of ignorance.

Several of the low-income, FGS felt like an outsider amongst their peers when they could not engage in seemingly inexpensive activities, particularly when section-mates would repeatedly inquire about the lack of participation.

Employment

In addition to feeling restricted from community-building or residence hall activities low-income students often felt constrained by their work schedules. One low-income, first generation student felt continually burdened by his/her workload, expressing that:

> Work-study is a means of meeting financial need at [college] which is better than nothing, but it's still a huge limitation. How much more might my academics excel if I wasn't spending hundreds of hours per semester working just to be here? How much would my social life improve?

As a result of heavy workloads on top of demanding academic schedules, these students had difficulty finding time to engage in extracurricular activities, which is another effective way to build a community on campus. FGS from low-income backgrounds tended to associate with individuals from similar class backgrounds whom they met through work, possibly resulting in a lack of diversity within social circles. First-generation, low-income students employed in high-visibility on-campus jobs such as the school cafeteria also felt less integrated into the student experience when confronted with the perception that they were serving their more privileged peers.

Advocacy and Support

At SLA College, a faculty member initiated an advocacy and support group for first-generation and low-income students. Nearly all of the students interviewed had been involved with the advocacy and support group in some capacity. Members of the group organized social activities for existing members and incoming freshman, helped students understand and take advantage of on-campus opportunities, and worked to identify and address the unique needs of first-generation and low-income students. The interviewed students expressed that the group generally had a positive impact on their college experience, particularly since it increased a sense of belonging and helped them collectively navigate the complex college system.

Recommendations

- Campus-Wide Awareness: *Incorporate class issues into freshman activities and discussions. Invite speakers who address class issues. Foster dialogue on campus by encouraging the disclosure and discussion of experiences related to socioeconomic background.*

- College-Sponsored Activities: *Organize or encourage community-building activities that are free of charge. Subsidize student involvement in varsity athletics or recreational activities if money poses an obstacle.*

- Residence Life Activities: *Ensure that Resident Assistants are sensitive to different socioeconomic backgrounds and how that may impact a student's sense of belonging or inclusion. Encourage discussions in residence halls regarding socioeconomic backgrounds to foster understanding. Organize activities that do not require a financial commitment.*

- First-Generation/Low-Income Students Support and Advocacy: *Encourage the creation of a support and advocacy group for low-income/FGS. Establish a mentorship program with faculty and staff who are first-generation or come from low-income backgrounds.*

Academic Environment

Respondents who self-identified as lower class expressed that they experienced significant academic challenges at SLA College due to their socioeconomic background. Only 33% percent of low-income students felt prepared for college academic expectations in comparison to 80% of their upper-class peers (See Figure 9). Not only did low-income students feel underprepared for college, but they were also more likely to disclose experiences of discrimination in the classroom. This section discusses the academic challenges particular to students from low-income backgrounds at SLA College.

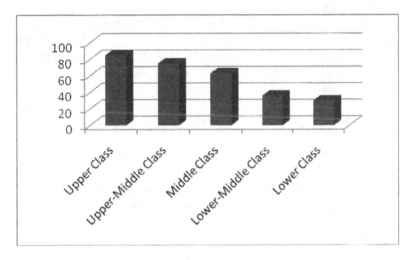

Figure 9. Academic Preparation

Access to Classes

Limited access to classes was one of the primary areas in which low-income, FGS felt inadvertently discriminated against at SLA College. Many classes require fees in order to participate, particularly classes that fulfill fine art credits. Nearly all of the FGS from low-income backgrounds indicated in interviews that class fees presented a barrier to their involvement. At SLA College, class fees and lab fees were not factored into the calculation of financial need, which resulted in diminished financial aid for those students who wanted to enroll in classes with fees. Furthermore, scholarships or waivers were not available to assist low-income students. One student expressed his/her feeling of exclusion:

> *By offering many wonderful opportunities such as art classes, [student recreation classes], science classes, etc without scholarship I feel that I have had fewer options in the kinds of activities I participate in at [this college].*

First-generation, low-income students felt like they had less breadth in their academic and personal pursuits as a result of restrictive fees. This obstacle limited academic opportunities for some students and may also have resulted in diminished classroom diversity.

Access to Resources

One of the biggest academic obstacles for low-income, FGS is the lack of financial resources necessary to purchase course materials. Although books and supplies are included in the calculation of financial need, low-income students still struggled to afford the books and resources necessary for classes. This finding is consistent throughout the research on FGS (Eitel & Martin, 2009; Lyons, 2004; Palmer, Pinto, & Parente, 2001). This may result from the fact that a student or family financial contribution was overestimated in relation to financial need. In some extreme instances, students were forced to choose between groceries or supplies. A handful of professors were sensitive to this difficulty and ensured that a copy of the materials for class were available in the student library. Some low-income, FGS felt comfortable requesting a copy of materials from professors, while another subset felt ashamed and were less likely to ask for help.

Classroom Sensitivity

Eighty percent of the low-income, FGS who were interviewed stated that they had felt uncomfortable during classroom conversations. In the survey three low-income students related specific experiences in the classroom in which their peers and/or professors were not considerate of class issues, particularly in regards to poverty and welfare. Respondents noted that classist statements made in open classroom discussion were not appropriately fielded by the professor. One student stated that "people make frequent comments both in and outside the classroom about how lazy and undeserving welfare recipients are." The student expressed that s/he took such comments as "a personal affront" because his/her family has been on state assistance, yet never felt empowered enough in the classroom or in social settings to talk about his/her personal views or background.

Recommendations

- Classroom sensitivity: *Improve communication on campus regarding class diversity and educational background. Openly acknowledge that the student body does not exclusively consist of upper (middle) class individuals. Provide better training for professors to deal with class issues and classism in the classroom. It would be valuable to assemble and discuss actual classroom experiences from students.*

- Books: *Require that all professors have a copy of the text to loan to students. Require that all texts be put on reserve at the library.*

- Technological resources: *Ensure that the college provides sufficient access to computers and other necessary technology, especially during the evenings.*

- Academic resources: *Advertise the academic resources available for students who feel underprepared. Acknowledge different educational backgrounds that result from socioeconomic disparities and how those may affect aptitude at the college level.*

- Class fees: *Incorporate additional class fees into financial aid calculations. Establish a scholarship fund to assist students.*

- Study abroad: *Provide financial assistance or waive the application fee for students who cannot afford the fee. Advertise resources to students, including the ability to help them find employment and apply for temporary work visas so that they can earn money abroad.*

Conclusion

Since the majority of FGS hail from low-income backgrounds, it is important to consider the impacts of socioeconomic status on college experiences, social acclimation and academic success. This study found that FGS from low-income backgrounds may discover institutional disparities that discourage, if not fully deter them from pursuing opportunities available to their peers. Students from low-income backgrounds are less likely to study abroad, engage in experiential learning courses (i.e., experiences that foster individual observation and interaction with educational subjects in non-classroom environments), enroll in classes that require fees, participate in residence hall activities, or pursue extracurricular activities due to their financial constraints.

Given the potential disparity in opportunities for low-income, FGS in academic institutions, the colleges that recruit and admit these students should evaluate whether they bear an additional responsibility to ensure that all students, regardless of financial capital, share equal access to academic and social experiences. While all institutional, academic and social challenges cannot be resolved immediately, college administrators, faculty and students should continually evaluate these issues as they seek to foster a fulfilling college experience for all students and define the future direction of their respective institutions.

References

Bourdieu, P. (1986). The Forms of Capital. In Richardson, J. G. (ed.) *Handbook of Theory and Research for the Sociology of Education.* Greenwood Press, New York, pp. 241-258.

Eitel, S., & Martin, J. (2009, June). First-generation female college students' financial literacy: real and perceived barriers to degree completion. *College Student Journal,* 189-199.

Horn, L., & Nunez, A. (2000). Mapping the road to college: First-generation students' math track, planning strategies, and context of support. *Education Statistics Quarterly, 2,* pp. 81-86.

Inman, W. E., & Mayes, L. (1999). The importance of being first: Unique characteristics of first-generation community college students. *Community College Review, 26(4),* pp. 3-22.

Lyons, A. (2004). A profile of financially at-risk college students. *The Journal of Consumer Affairs, 38(1),* 56-80.

Palmer, T., Pinto, M., & Parente, D. (2001). College students' credit card debit and the role of parental involvement: Implications for public policy. *Journal of Public Policy and Marketing, 20(1),* 105-113.

Pike, G., & Kuh, G. (2005). First- and second-generation college students: A comparison of their engagement and intellectual development. *The Journal of Higher Education, 76,* 276-300.

Terenzini, P. T., Springer, L, Yaeger, P. M., Pascarella, E. T., & Nora, A. (1996). First-generation college students: Characteristics, experiences, and cognitive development. *Research in Higher Education, 37(1),* pp. 1-22.

CHAPTER SEVEN

OPPORTUNITIES AND CHALLENGES IN A UNIVERSITY-LEVEL PROGRAM FOR FIRST-GENERATION STUDENTS

Keith Nainby

Those of us working in higher education, whether as faculty, staff, or administrators, increasingly find ourselves working with students described as "first-generation college students" who, demographically speaking, are pursuing more extensive educational paths than other, older members of their family. Indeed, these more extensive educational paths—usually college and university degree or certificate programs—often take first-generation college students into situations (both in and outside the classroom) that they will not have encountered before, neither in their homes nor in the communities of work, play, church, and so on that have been typical in their own neighborhoods.

For me, for example, as a first-generation college student, coming home for holidays meant more than just leaving my friends and professors and spending time, instead, with my parents and siblings. It meant that the books on the shelves, which for my parents included almost nothing but popular novels, were quite different than the variety of books I was surrounded by at college. The films, plays, and concerts that were discussed by my peers at college weren't available to me, or others in my neighborhood, during the times that I was at home. When, as a first-semester freshman, I was invited to the middle-class home of a psychology professor, there was wine served with our meal; it wasn't the fact that I was legally underage that made this a striking and unusual experience for me, it was the fact that I'd never been at a table inside a person's home where wine was served. My parents did not even own wine glasses. My claim is not that I was suddenly thrown into confusion by the presence of wine inside a middle–class home; on the contrary, it was just the sort of contrast to my own home that I had tacitly expected. But what is significant, for me, is the felt sense of trepidation I had that I would do something wrong, such as hold the glass wrong, drink too quickly, or—even more likely, I imagined—be so concerned about mimicking the holding or the drinking of others that I would be obvious about it, that I would be "found out" as an imposter.

Reflecting on experiences like these, in conjunction with literature on the challenges facing first–generation college students, has led me to question my own practices as a university professor (Bowles & Gintis, 1976; Willis, 1977; Apple, 1979). Specifically, I am interested in two related sets of questions about the ways that FGS encounter life at my university: (1) What kinds of cultural expectations, norms, and values exist within the university setting, and how do these differ from the expectations, norms and values of our students' disparate backgrounds? Which of these differences are clear and recognizable to students and other members of the university community, and which are only dimly understood or even obscured within the "typical" interactions of the university? (2) Given that such cultural differences exist for our FGS, and given that cultural differences only become successfully negotiated over time and in process (if at all), how might these students be stymied in educational projects because of this cultural knowledge gap? How might they be marginalized within scholarly communities for similar reasons?

Researchers who have pursued similar questions have found evidence that such culture gaps do, in fact, affect students at all levels of education, including colleges and universities. These effects are felt through such institutionalized practices as: curriculum development that canonizes specific authors and specific types of knowledge; calendaring courses, programs and events in ways that normalize middle–class job schedules and cultural forms; teacher–centered pedagogical strategies; competitive grading and class ranking; and campus support systems (textbook selection, the sale of education–related goods and services, campus–based eateries) that depend on consumer capitalism. Moreover, the operation of these forces that work to socialize FGS into middle–class culture is not merely confined to formal institutional practices; it extends to student affiliation groups, time usage decisions, and—perhaps most importantly—informal interaction among students, teachers, staff, and administrators. Indeed, such informal modes of interaction are just as important as legitimated institutional forms in shaping the acculturation process in college and university settings.

In recent decades in the California State University system, one significant institutional effort has attempted to provide unique support to FGS, especially those from cultural and/or economic circumstances that may not have served them in ideal ways as "future college/university students" prior to their entry into the CSU (our program mission statement describes such students as "educationally disadvantaged"). This program is called the Faculty Mentor Program, and its goal is to attend as directly as possible to both the acculturation process of FGS and the informal interaction modes that such students develop among students, faculty, and staff.

At CSU Stanislaus, FMP features three distinct modes of structured engagement of "educationally disadvantaged" students: (1) (Student) Protégé and (faculty/staff) Mentor one–to–one pairings intended to foster Protégés' developing ability to create and sustain interpersonal support systems within the university setting, and to provide Protégés with specific resources they might utilize both academically and personally to negotiate challenges in their changing lives; (2) Large–scale, structured interactions among those involved in the program, which foreground an explicit pedagogical goal (such as themed programs on time management, goal–setting, networking, etc.); (3) Large–scale, collective cultural experiences designed to expand the sphere of Protégés' cultural access (trips to local theatre productions, culturally themed sharing of food, dance, and music, etc.).

As a member of the Board of Directors of FMP at CSU Stanislaus and as a first–generation college student myself, I find evidence of both meaningful success and significant remaining challenges as I reflect on the FMP process and its role in our university. The most important successes, of course, are evident not merely in enhanced retention and graduation rates among FMP protégés relative to the general student population (a point of pride for our program, given that these are "educationally disadvantaged" students), but in the strength of the relational support among protégés and mentors across the program. "Relational support" is not easy to measure in objective outcomes, though the retention and graduation rates provide suggestive, if not conclusive, evidence of this support structure. Instead, FMP strives to attend to more subjective evidence of the positive impact of the program. We have established feedback loops for both Protégés and Mentors at the program level through printed survey responses, and these supplement narratives that survive within the program through our deep connection to long–standing Mentors who preserve program history as well as to Protégé alumni. To show how this program helps to support students with less access to educational culture, I will discuss each of the three modes of engagement in turn.

(1) Protégés greatly enhance their access to information such as scholarship programs, counseling services, career opportunities, research teams, and on–campus organizations and activities through the one–to–one relationship with a Mentor. This type of access is invaluable. In my own experience as a FGS at a large university, I found myself cut off from many of these networks despite the fact that I was only on campus because of a scholarship award. In contrast, our Protégés, through pairing one–to–one with a faculty Mentor, have an initial contact point within the university structure in the form of an individual person with whom the Protégé has, or is developing, an interpersonal rapport. This interpersonal relationship is initiated by the Protégé, as a condition of participation in the program. Thus, the challenge to "approach a Mentor," which can be an obstacle for many students and which can slow a student's effort to integrate into university culture, becomes an immediate opportunity for success for prospective Protégés, a way of taking a kind of structured first step. This has the iterative positive consequence of making the one–to–one relationship one more likely to be founded on trust, as the Mentor within the relationship has been, initially, approached face to face and directly asked to serve. This is a rather more ethically immediate connection than I had with any of my own undergraduate professors or advisors. Three specific examples of how these one–to–one relationships shape student lives follow.

(A) I am working with one Protégé who, as a member of our university Honors program, has to make a series of difficult decisions regarding her course scheduling and graduation timetable because of the unique constraints of the Honors program. These decisions involved such choices as whether or not to delay graduation, how to frame a transcript for her planned future graduate study, how her own spiritual commitments outside the university affected her graduation timetable, and so on. Despite the smaller relative size of the Honors program, this student, who I know also as an in–class student from one of my courses, tends not to speak much in class and, as a result, does not make contact with professors easily. As a result, she did not have a more experienced person with whom to sort out the complexities of her own goals as they rubbed against the constraints of the Honors program; a traditional academic advisor may not have known this Protégé's unique perspective well enough to support her scheduling efforts. Yet these forms of advice are precisely the forms that students from more educationally privileged families will often seek from parents and/or family friends.

(B) One of the aspects of FMP that we point to with the greatest pride is the opportunity our Protégés have to develop more direct academic collaborations with professors. In the Spring of 2009, two Stanislaus FMP Protégés working on two separate research projects, one in Chemistry and one in Biology, were awarded prizes within the top two in their respective categories in a CSU–wide undergraduate research competition. This is part of an ongoing, sustained effort within FMP to integrate Protégés into the scholarly community through direct collaboration on projects, which will not only help these Protégés develop their technical and academic skills, but also prepare them to succeed in post–baccalaureate programs.

(C) A more material consequence of one–to–one relationships in the past has involved connecting several of our Protégés with economic needs to a program on campus that provides short–term loans for students who are in the midst of a pressing cycle involving rent, books, and so on. Though many colleges and universities have such programs, especially connected with financial aid offices, the availability of short–term loans is not always very widely publicized (for understandable reasons) and is precisely the sort of resource that a one–to–one relationship can highlight for an individual Protégé. The dimension of trust in the Protégé–Mentor relationship is vital in this situation, because for many FGS a lack of money is associated with shame (this was certainly true in my case as a young person among wealthier peers). In these situations, there is often little chance that—outside an interpersonal relationship founded on trust rather than on institutional roles and responsibilities—many FGS would be able to ask the necessary questions of a series of anonymous staff that it would take to apply for a loan. Veteran Mentors narrate similar experiences with respect to other university resources such as the counseling center or the ombudsperson's office.

In sum, the one–to–one connection that each FMP Protégé makes with a faculty Mentor gives her/him a broader, more interpersonally grounded set of pathways through which to "get it," the "it" in this case being the cultural values and habits of communication and organization necessary to enhance their access to academic and professional opportunities. Academics and professionals working in higher education and related fields are often in the process of building, developing, and maintaining just such support structures for FGS, and I find that FMP enriches that effort. Indeed, this form of interpersonal intervention is crucial because much of the so–called "gap" between FMP Protégés and more traditional, middle–class students from college–educated families has accrued through a series of interpersonal interactions, from families to workplaces to schools. Thus, an interpersonal intervention, in some of the ways shown in the prior examples, is often necessary to make a difference for FGS.

(2) In the second mode of engagement within FMP, Protégés and Mentors participate together in program–generated curricular workshops and training activities. These have taken place, in recent years, at both on–campus locations during time intervals ranging from two to four hours, and at off–campus locations one time each academic year for a three–day, intensive series of projects. Topics in recent years have included: strategies for long– and short–term goal setting and goal monitoring, including time management; understanding fear responses and learning to confront these, in academic and personal contexts; recognizing conditions of change and responding to these through forecasting and strategic planning; and developing the interpersonal and intrapersonal skills required for professional and social networking. As this list suggests, topics are chosen with regard for the forms of cultural knowledge that may often be "left out" for students whose prior experiences may not have included middle–class academic or professional communities.

One outcome of these efforts, beyond the development of Protégés' academic and interpersonal skills, that is easy to overlook but is a major benefit of FMP is the cross–fertilization of pedagogical and interpersonal strategies for working more effectively with FGS. I find this especially critical working on a campus that is culturally, ethnically, and linguistically diverse, because there remains so much for me to learn in order to be the kind of pedagogical resource that each unique student deserves in a professor. Through participating in FMP workshops like those described above, I have come to better understand what resources students on my campus may be relying on in their pursuit of academic success, and what resources they may not yet have developed. This leads me to attend more sensitively than I had before, in preparing lessons and in facilitating classroom discussion and activities, to students' needs and expectations.

(3) In the third mode of engagement within FMP, larger groups of Protégés and Mentors attend selected cultural events together; those events with an associated entry cost are paid for with FMP programming dollars. These have included, in recent years, Yosemite National Park; plays (both on and off campus); yoga and martial arts programs; sporting events; and concerts. One of my own experiences with such an event confirmed, for me, the value of these efforts: I shared, with twelve Protégés as well as several Mentors, a trip in Spring 2009 to a play at a community in a medium–sized city about forty–five miles away from our university. During our trip, I learned that for more than half of this group of Protégés, this was the first play they had seen, and for several of them it was their first trip to this particular city. This led to further conversation about the large cities in the San Francisco Bay area, which is approximately ninety miles from our university; in that conversation, I learned that four of these Protégés had never been to any of the cities in the Bay area. This has helped to spur additional discussions for future programming events in larger cities. Such opportunities are invaluable in broadening the social, cultural, and civic perspectives of students with limited resources for travel.

Yet despite these benefits, FMP faces three significant challenges as we move forward at our institution. These challenges, unsurprisingly, stem directly from resource constraints that flow through institutions (such as the California State University system) as a result of economic scarcity and our history of privileging competitive standards of success. In other words, our program faces challenges that parallel the very constraints that often shape the lives of FGS. The three closely related challenges we face are:

(1) We cannot grow, as a program, unless we continue to recruit and train new faculty mentors. This is because the values of the program demand that mentors and protégés have the time and focus necessary to develop and sustain meaningful one–to–one relationships, relationships that are unfairly strained when the protégé–mentor ratio gets too high. The anonymity and alienation that first–generation college students often experience is what our program is most carefully designed to prevent, and yet the ever–increasing demands on faculty for larger class sizes and more research productivity are making it harder each year to successfully recruit new mentors. Mentors within the program are volunteering their time, both to

participate in large–scale FMP interactions and to serve as a one–to–one Mentor for (typically) multiple Protégés. We strive, as a program, to identify for prospective Mentors the value of their service, not only for particular students but also for the university as a whole and for each faculty member as an individual. For me, this value has included enhanced opportunities to shape my pedagogy, as I described earlier; increased connections with faculty across departments and colleges, faculty who I otherwise would not likely have known; and much greater understanding of university programs and resources that I have gained through sharing with Protégés and other Mentors.

But benefits of this sort require initial commitment to relational processes. It is difficult, within the current culture of "objective measures" and "evidence" that persists in higher education, to make these benefit immediately recognizable to faculty members whose resources are already stretched thin, and who are encouraged by the institutionalized retention process to compartmentalize their efforts among the "research/teaching/service" rubric. According to this logic, the most obvious way to account for the "return" on one's investment of time and energy in FMP is as "service," which is the category least likely to prove an obstacle to retention, promotion or tenure at most institutions. In this way, the prevailing logic of competitively distinguishing oneself, through peer–reviewed journal publications and conference presentations (in research) or Likert–scale surveys of students (in teaching) can dissuade prospective Mentors from devoting resources to a collaborative, process–based program like FMP.

One way we could more effectively recruit, even within prevailing retention logics at universities, would be to: (2) raise the profile of our program within our particular institution. The need to raise one's profile is a problem facing many programs dedicated to the success of FGS because, again, academic culture has historically been grounded in highlighting competitive successes—through ranked grading and GPAs, grants, and awards. I have tried, in this essay, to offer some accounts of success within our program. At our university, we have also had some success in raising our profile, because in addition to narrative measures of outcomes we are able to offer some objective measures as well, through tracking retention data, graduation rates, academic honors, awards like the research awards noted earlier, and so on. I would characterize our program, within the university structure as a whole, as relatively well affirmed by university administration, historically speaking. And yet there is a fundamental philosophical conflict embedded in our efforts to become something like a "marquee" program on campus: a program that is designed to serve students who have existed at the margins, academically and culturally, would necessarily lose itself were it to become lauded as an example of "excellence" in and of itself. Identifying any one program, or any single group of students, as "excellent" by definition underscores the "ordinariness" of other programs, of other students. In this way, striving for distinction recreates the very hierarchical logic that both privileges certain forms of knowledge (those that enable one to "excel") and makes some of those forms invisible (those that become "ordinary"). So the unique challenge facing programs like FMP that serve students at the margins is that we must raise our profile by calling into question, at least in some contexts, the very measures of excellence we also hope to promote among our own Protégés. This paradoxical necessity, sharing codes of power while at the same time calling them into question, has been recognized by scholars such as Lorde (1984) and Delpit (2006) as a part of the process of transforming social structures that might otherwise preserve inequalities. Within university settings in which resources for all programs are scarce, this is a particularly acute burden for programs like FMP.

Finally, given the specter of inequality that persists throughout our efforts, we come to the issue that is at the core of the relationship of FGS to higher education as a historical vehicle of access: money. Like many similar programs, FMP faces the constant battle of: (3) securing stable funding from institutional and other sources for the continuation of our work. This is an increasing challenge for departments and programs of all kinds across the landscape of higher education, given two disturbing trends: (A) declining public support for higher education in the form of state spending as a proportion of overall tax revenue, and (B) political pressure to "standardize" educational outcomes within post–secondary schools, which leads to centralization of resources and thereby tends to siphon resources away from innovative programs, like FMP, that are difficult to standardize. Those of us at public colleges and universities who devote some of our attention to the experiences of FGS must continue working to identify the value of programs like FMP. Doing so can have two potential positive outcomes related to securing stable funding: First, it can help establish our relevance within our institutions, making funding these programs a priority for administrators. Second, it can heighten awareness of our work outside our institutions, for prospective donors in the community. My hope is that this essay can add to the voices striving to achieve these goals.

References

Apple, M. (1979). *Ideology and curriculum.* Boston: Routledge & Kegan Paul.

Bowles, S., & Gintis, H. (1976). *Schooling in capitalist America: Educational reform and the contradictions of economic life.* New York: Basic Books.

Delpit, L. (2006). *Other people's children: Cultural conflict in the classroom.* New York: New York.

Lorde, A. (1984). *Sister outsider: Essays and speeches.* Berkeley: Crossing P.

Willis, P. (1977). *Learning to labor: How working class kids get working class jobs.* Lexington, KY: D.C. Heath.

◆ CHAPTER EIGHT ◆

CREATING LIVING AND LEARNING COMMUNITIES THAT ENGAGE OUR FIRST-GENERATION STUDENTS: SUGGESTIONS FOR POLICY AND PRACTICE

Rita L. Rahoi-Gilchrest, Sarah Olcott, and Ron Elcombe

Establishing learning communities is not unusual; as one educator notes, "Learning communities are now part of the vocabulary of Higher Education" (Tinto, n/a, cited online by Washington Center, n/a); some have been in place for decades (Washington Center, n/a). Interest in learning communities is underlined by The Policy Center on the First Year of College, which observed in its 2002 survey of first-year academic practices that "the enrolling of at least some cohorts of students into two or more courses (i.e., a learning community) is common practice at approximately 62% of institutions. But it is still rare for learning communities to involve more than 50% of first-year students" (2002, p. 2). And establishing learning communities at an institution with a high rate of incoming FGS's is less common—and more complex—still. At Winona State University, a small Midwestern campus located in Minnesota approximately two hours southeast of the Twin Cities, the challenge of creating effective learning communities is combined with meeting the unique needs of a high FGS population to engage more than 800 first- and second-year students residing at the university's West Campus.

Based on experience with this program, we present suggestions intended to help establish policy and practice for establishing successful living and learning communities with FGS populations. Beginning with observations about the FGS population served at Winona State as well as a brief history of our LLC (Living and Learning Communities) program, we then review relevant prior research on the connection between LLC participation and perceived student engagement/retention. We move next to summarizing the research conducted at WSU on the effectiveness of the LLC initiative, and finally close with observations about the challenges in establishing LLC initiatives that truly draw on both the academic and residential aspects of our FGS's college experience.

Getting to Know Our Students and Our LLC Program— A Brief History

At the Winona State University West Campus, where the LLC programs are housed, our students in 2008 were 44.3% male and 55.7% female; they were primarily from Minnesota (59.6%), Wisconsin (29.9%), and Illinois (5.4%), with 5.1% reporting a permanent address from other states or countries. The majority (20%) had not declared a major; of those students who had declared, Education and Nursing were the most popular choices (Lopez, Merkouris, & Olcott, 2008).

Not surprisingly, given the number of students who come to WSU from the upper Midwest, our overall numbers of FGS's are quite high. Across data collected from Fall 2004–2007 from the background information survey all incoming students complete, as compiled by Assessment and Institutional Research, students reporting neither parent had a four-year degree averaged 42.92% (see Figure 1; see also Appendix A).

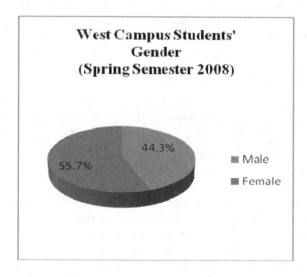

Figure 1. West Campus Students by Gender

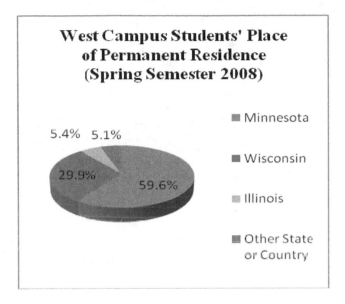

Figure 2. Place of permanent residence

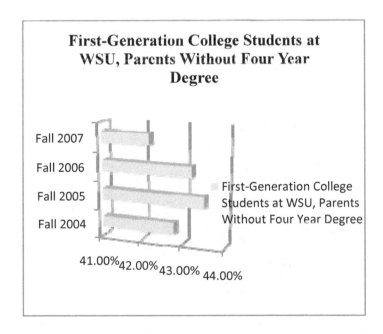

Figure 3. Numbers of FGS's at WSU; Parents without four-year degree

Clearly, the numbers of students at our campus who need insight into what to expect from a four-year institution or degree are worth noting. Having provided a global sense of our incoming student population, we can now describe the Living and Learning Communities (LLC) program designed to meet the needs of this at-risk population.

Housed within Winona State University's Residential College at its West Campus (comprised of three residence halls—Lourdes, Tau, and Maria), the LLC program is designed to help to transition first-year students (including many FGS's) to college life by connecting them to a faculty member who is interested in them and shares their interest in a particular academic/topic area. Comparisons of the numbers of FGS's across the entire campus with the Residential College generally, and then students enrolled in the LLCs (all of whom take the RESC201 class), reveal that the numbers of FGS's in both the Residential College (44.44% from Fall 2006-Fall 2009) and the LLCs (47.87% from Fall 2007-Fall 2009) are slightly higher than the campus average of 42.92%, shown as follows:

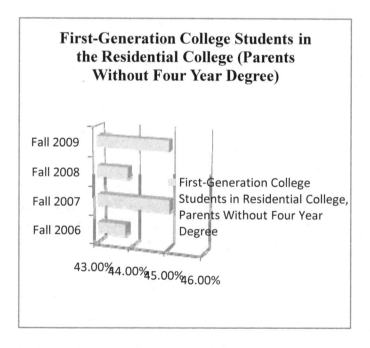

Figure 4. Numbers of FGS's in the Residential College; Parents without four-year degree

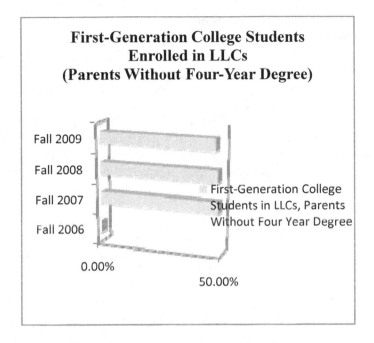

First-Generation College Students
Enrolled in LLCs
(Parents Without Four-Year Degree)

Fall 2009

Fall 2008

Fall 2007

First-Generation College
Students in LLCs, Parents
Without Four Year Degree

Fall 2006

0.00%

50.00%

Figure 5. Numbers of FGS's enrolled in LLCs; Parents without four-year degree

The Residential College program currently operates nine LLCs, each consisting of 4-5 courses that are linked on a theme. Each LLC includes a 'Connections' 1-credit, activity-based course, as well as 3-4 University Studies courses that help to fulfill the student's general education requirements. From Fall 2007–Fall 2008, the themes included Curiosity, Exploration–Career & Life Choices, Entrepreneurship, Gender & Culture, Global Village, Mississippi River, Native Pathways, and Whose Planet is it Anyway?, It's Political, The Savvy Adventure Traveler, and Creative Expressions. Besides the Living and Learning Communities, program offerings in the Residential College also include an Emerging Leaders' Retreat, a student-run coffeehouse ("Mugshots"), a collegiate house system and numerous building/house programs. To put this program in perspective among the many such initiatives in place, we next review some of the more recent studies on living and learning communities and their impact on student attrition and retention.

Putting Our Program in Context—
Prior Studies of Living and Learning Communities

Research in higher education consistently indicates student attrition can be caused by lack of academic and social engagement. Living and learning communities have been developed in response to these findings to increase student involvement and satisfaction, to connect in and out of classroom learning, to foster a sense of community in the residence halls, as well as to encourage student engagement. By being involved in an interdisciplinary and interactive community, students are introduced to multifaceted, diverse perspectives that encourage critical thinking and contextual learning (Kuh & Zhao, 2004).

Living and learning communities (LLCs) have been linked to positive behaviors such as increased academic effort, openness to diversity, social tolerance, and both intrapersonal and personal development, as Smith (2003) commented:

> The most recent National Survey of Student Engagement, for example, found that participation in learning communities was positively related to diversity experiences, student gains in personal and social development, practical competence, general education, and overall satisfaction with the undergraduate college experience. (p. 3)

Minkler (2002) stated that "the results of over a decade of research on LLCs indicate that there are definite benefits seen in student retention, student satisfaction with classes, increased student success, and intellectual development" (p. 8). Pascarella, Terenzini and Bliming (1994) reported that in a residential or living and learning community the "central theme appears to be one of bringing about a closer integration of the student's living environment with his or her academic environment" (p. 32). Compared to students who live off-campus, residential students have significantly higher levels of faculty-student interaction and peer support, greater academic and social integration, and significantly greater satisfaction and commitment (Pascarella, Terenzini, & Bliming). Kuh and Zhao (2004) validate this, finding learning communities were associated with student gains in personal and social development, and practical competence.

When comparing students in a living and learning community to traditional residence hall students, Inkelas, Vogt, Longerbeam, Owen, and Johnson (2006) found LLC students were statistically "more likely to have a mentoring relationship with faculty and were more likely to go beyond basic interactions with faculty" (p.3). LLC students also had significantly more positive perceptions of their residence hall climates (both academically and socially) and viewed the campus climate for racial and ethnic diversity as positive. Additionally, "specific academic and intellectual benefits of the LLC program participation for students of color, non-Christian, and gay, lesbian, and bisexual students were found" in a 2005 study (Pasque & Murphy, 2005, p. 2).

Additionally, several scholars have noted LLCs hold special promise for reaching FGS's. Thayer (2000) identified LLCs as one of the ways to enhance both community-building and academic focus for FGS's. Also, Tinto (1998) claimed that LLCs help FGS's form peer groups that support them well beyond the classroom and increase learning. The University of Cincinnati is taking this into account by implementing its new "Gen-1" LLC/theme house in 2008 designed specifically to offer support and services to first-generation college students (Fuller, 2008). And, responding to President Obama's recent call to help make college possible for all students, the "First in the Family" organization is promoting FGS's on video talking about how living and learning communities support them in gaining their four-year degrees (First in the Family, n/d). For FGS's, who often lack perspective on the realities of the college experience, as well as for students across the board, LLCs provide another means of enhancing satisfaction, engagement, and retention. With this in mind, we now move to our own research on WSU's LLCs and their influence/impact on our FGS population.

Research into the LLC Program—
What We Have Found So Far

In April 2008, a study was conducted to examine the satisfaction and engagement of students who live on West Campus at Winona State University. The analysis found a statistically significant difference in the answers of students who were in an LLC compared to those who did not take advantage of that opportunity. The hypothesis was that the students involved in the living and learning communities would have significantly different answers to some of the survey statements than the students who were not involved in living and learning communities. The prediction was that in the areas of out-of-classroom experiences with faculty, educational activities, interactions with faculty and staff, and connecting with other students at the West Campus, the LLC students would rate their engagement and satisfaction higher.

As the first step in this research project, focus groups were held on Winona State University's Assessment Day. A total of 17 students participated. Questions which were focused on students' academic and social experiences in the halls, as well as their interactions with faculty and staff, were asked. The data was collected in three steps. First the focus group sessions were recorded and transcribed by the person facilitating the discussion. Second, the transcripts were reviewed in an effort to find common themes among the information provided by students. Finally, common themes were elaborated by direct quotes from students. In reviewing the focus group transcripts, we observed several recurring themes, which are reviewed in the following section, as well as samples of students' actual observations.

One recurring theme that was mentioned by students was a feeling that the Residential College, or West Campus (where the Residential College is located), felt like a home away from home. Some of the comments recorded in the focus groups related to this theme were:

—It's like you're getting away from school, and you're still here obviously, but it feels like you're going home at the end of the day.

—It is a home away from home over here and that is what I like best about it.

—I think it's definitely a great social experience because you're coming home at the end of the day. There's that feeling of, you get on the bus, you leave class behind you, you still have homework ahead of you, but you leave that classroom behind you . . . if I'm going to hang out with friends, if I want to do homework with friends, it's more of a social environment, not to say that academics aren't important and emphasized, but it gives that feeling of we all kind of live in a community.

—I definitely like the separation of the academic life and the social life . . . for me, if I were on main campus, I think I would be stressed out more about classes because you could see the academic building and it's always looming over you, whereas when you come back [here], you're able to remove yourself from that situation, and step into your social and personal life, away from the barriers of the buildings of academic life.

As indicated by these statements, many students felt a sense of community or a sense of family with other students in the Residential College or on West Campus. Here were some other direct quotes from students who spoke candidly about this sense of community in the focus groups:

—This year, as the resident assistant, I enjoy the community that I've been able to establish on my floor, my residents have a sense of family among them and they definitely interact with each other in a great way . . . I think that's really been important to me.
—The sense of community and the home away from home aspect. I just think that like people on West campus, I don't know if they are nicer, but I feel more of a connection with them. I guess because I am with them more.
—I don't know, just talking to people that lived on main [campus], I feel like they don't have quite that same sense of community as we do here.

Several students indicated that they felt residents of West Campus had a closer relationship with each other due not only to proximity, but also due to taking classes, studying, riding the bus, and going to programs together. Students also indicated that while they liked the separation from the academic buildings on main campus, they felt it was easier for them to go 'home' (as they described West Campus) and work on their homework. Students also reported that they felt that their residence hall was an academic experience because they took classes, studied, and socialized with other students living on West Campus. This theme was revealed by these comments:

—I think living in the halls provides sort of an academic support system because everybody here is a student, so they're going through the same thing. And so when you . . . come across a bunch of people studying, you feel like you should also sit down and focus on your academics.
—I think it helps when you come home from classes and everyone else is studying, so you study too or take the bus over to the library you do it all together. It is more fun because I do it with the people in my hall.
—I participated in the residential college theme my freshman year, and that program was really nice to get me started with the basic people that I knew, because I had a couple classes with the same people, and then we had our themed class, too, once a week. So my early base of friends and people that I knew were established . . . so that was really nice.

—I think if I lived on main [campus] I would just be trying to get away from campus. So, I think West campus has more of an academic appeal because I am more willing to start on homework because I feel comfortable over here, so I am more willing to do it because I really enjoy that. I think I do better.

—By living in Tau, we have the rotunda, and so you have a nice quiet study area, where you do not have to go to main campus or to the library, but you still have that academic retreat place where you can go and study and feel like you're accomplishing something.

In summary, then:

- Students had a common feeling that the Residential College, or West Campus where the Residential College is located, felt like a home away from home. This finding is particularly essential in dealing with FGS's, since college is an even less familiar environment than for students whose families have college degrees and have given them a sense of what to expect.

- Students felt that students on West Campus had a closer relationship with each other due to the fact that they took classes, studied with, rode the bus with, lived with, and went to programs with students who lived in the same buildings as them. For FGS's, these connections are key to retention as they can help replace the missing support network of families and friends.

- Students saw the Residence Life staff (student staff and both Hall Directors) and Residential College staff (Residential College Director and Program Coordinator) as highly visible at evening programming and events, but reported that they rarely saw faculty at evening programming with the exception of activities that were held in conjunction with their respective living and learning community. For FGS's, faculty presence is even more vital so students see role models of successful college graduates they lack at home.

Additionally, students reported that they preferred to take LLC classes when possible. For FGS's, classes that engage their personal interests or speak to their lived experience (for instance, the Mississippi River theme) can provide an easier transition to more

The focus groups were followed up with a paper survey administered to all West Campus students at their last floor meeting in April

2008. 489 surveys were collected, which represented 73.3% of the students living on the west campus at the time the survey was administered. Out of the 489 participants, 190 respondents (38.9%) were male and 299 (61.1%) were female. Among survey participants, 29.2% (143) of them were involved in the living and learning communities in fall 2000.

The Likert-type scale used in this survey asked the student to rate their *engagement* levels from never to very frequently on a five-point scale for 14 statements. The *satisfaction* section of the survey asked the students to rate their satisfaction on a five-point scale from not applicable to very satisfied on 10 statements. The survey has been included as Appendix C of this document. Statements were created after looking at many other surveys from online sources including the NSSE, with a goal of writing statements that any student at the Residential College could answer to see if the populations differed. The survey was administered in the last floor meeting over the week of April 16, 2008. This end of the year floor meeting was mandatory, but the students were told the survey was optional. For any student that missed the meeting, the Resident Assistants followed up with the student with the closing information and the survey.

The return rate for the survey was excellent with a 73.3% completion rate by students living on West Campus at the time the survey was administered. 65.1% of males living on the West Campus at the time the survey was administered took the survey and 79.7% of females living on the West Campus at the time the survey was administered took the survey.

Out of the 489 students that took the survey, 190 (38.9%) were male and 299 (61.1%) were female. These percentages were only a few points off from the actual percentages of males and females living on West Campus respectively 43.8% and 56.2%. The survey results were therefore representative of the student population on West Campus in regards to gender.

The majority of the students who lived on West Campus were first year students (82.2%). 29.2% (143) of students who filled out the survey were involved in the Living and Communities, which was very similar to the overall percentage of students in the LLCs for Fall 2007 (33.5%, or 270 respondents). Overall our response rate and demographic breakdown represented the actual population on West Campus. The results were able to be inferred to the population with a high degree of certainty; as noted earlier, the FGS rates are even higher at the Residential College and in the LLCs than the overall campus average.

In summary, the findings of the **engagement** statements included on the student survey are as follows. There was a significant difference between responses from students who did participate in the Living and Learning Communities compared to those who did not for all of the following items in the *End of the Year Survey of West Campus Students:*

1. Participate in out of classroom experiences with faculty (fieldtrips, speakers, projects).
2. Attend educational speakers, seminars, movie or retreats on West Campus.
6. Work with faculty and staff on committees, clubs or programs outside of classroom activities.
10. Use lounges to relax or hang out on West Campus.
12. Attend West Campus activities such as Winter Formal, Mugshots, Condom Bingo, etc.
13. Attend floor events.
14. Attend Hall Council.

The results indicated overall that there was a greater frequency of engagement for LLC students as compared to those who did not take part in the program.

There was a significant difference between the satisfaction reported by those who participated in living and learning communities and those who did not participate in living and learning communities for the following statements in the *End of the Year Survey of West Campus Students:*

1. The educational activities on West Campus (speakers, workshops, retreats, presentations, etc).
5. With your interactions with faculty on West Campus.

The results indicated greater satisfaction among LLC students for these areas as compared to those who did not take part in the program.

The results of this survey suggested that the Residential College living and learning communities were doing what they were intended to do, make connections; the data affirmed that the first year, first semester experience in a living learning community resulted in more frequent faculty-student interactions and greater participation in out-of classroom activities (both educational and social). Students involved in living and learning communities were also more connected to the physical spaces within their learning environment.

The fact that students self-select into the living and learning communities could be a factor in the results. Perhaps students that self-selected were joiners from the beginning; perhaps, since nearly 50% were FGS's, they found the creation of a contained community appealing. The general satisfaction and engagement information from this study have provided a baseline for future research on the LLC initiative.

As a final measure, we tracked retention and GPA statistics for LLC participants from Fall 2007, reported as follows:

Course Name	Students	Retained	Retention Rate	GPA
ResCol Seminar: Curiosity	31	23	74.19	2.66
ResCol Seminar: Exploration– Career & Life Choices	44	37	84.09	2.94
ResCol Seminar: Entrepreneurship	46	27	58.70	2.80
ResCol Seminar: Gender & Culture	22	17	77.27	2.91
ResCol Seminar: Global Village	31	21	67.74	3.18
ResCol Seminar: Mississippi River	42	33	78.57	3.00
ResCol Seminar: Native Pathways	4	3	75.00	3.48
ResCol Seminar: Whose Planet is it Anyway?	21	15	71.43	3.09

Figure 6. Retention and GPA Statistics Fall 2007 to Fall 2008

Of the 250 students enrolled in the eight LLC courses offered Fall 2007, 241 were New Entering Freshmen (NEF). 176 of those 241 were enrolled on the 10th day of term for a retention rate of 73.0%. Overall, the retention rate for Fall 2007 NEF students was 73.5%. Average GPA for the LLC cohort was 2.94, compared to an overall average GPA for the total retained Fall 2007 incoming freshmen. Therefore, there was no indication that the LLCs resulted in a significantly different retention rate or GPA; however, there is also some indication that some themes were more 'successful' than others. If this is taken into account, these numbers would look significantly different—a point to be discussed later in this chapter.

Lessons Learned:
Establishing Policy and Practice for LLCs for FGS's
We should clarify that the present Residential College program has gone through a variety of approaches in seeking to engage and educate our incoming FGS's. The program has variously offered special interest courses with resources/funding to identify and work on a shared problem or concern, heavily emphasizing service learning (the Yard Series, mentioned earlier); a full semester of courses students take on a single topic (such as the Native Pathways and Mississippi River series); linking cohorts of students in two connected basic courses (from English, speech, and math); and its current version, a one-credit 'Connections' course on a given theme, linked to enrollment in sections of our general education courses designed to further develop students' understanding of that theme (for instance, Entrepreneurship students learn about networking and interviewing, and are encouraged to give presentations on business and entrepreneurship-related topics in their public speaking course). Generally, we have found that the more 'intensive' Living and Learning Community approaches (the Yard Series) seem to students to require more effort than their 'normal' general education coursework; students do not at present perceive enough added value to enroll in those kinds of program options. Particularly for FGS's, who are already often apprehensive about their ability to do college-level work, this kind of approach can be intimidating. Therefore, **our first lesson learned has been:** *Take the many possible models for/ideas on LLCs and modify them to the current levels and needs of our FGS's.*

Also, since a number of our students come to us from relatively small towns and communities, students are not always comfortable in cohort programs if they include co-enrollment in linked courses.

The perception can be that this is 'too much like high school,' where students felt limited by being in many of the same classes together. *The second lesson: Balance the comfort of cohort programs (especially in a residential college) with relative independence in course selection and the ability to interact with non-FGS's outside of the LLCs.*

Many of our majors, such as education and nursing, require extremely regimented enrollment processes if a student is going to complete the major within a reasonable amount of time. In Minnesota, this issue was recently accentuated when the legislature mandated movement to 120-credit degree programs across all state universities. *A third lesson: LLCs will not work for all students in all degree programs; FGS's who are challenged by the stringent requirements of certain majors might have even more difficulty if they try to participate in LLCs.*

The successes of the program are also worth noting as we consider the lessons learned. Highly creative and innovative programs, such as the Mississippi River LLC, attract students who want a unique experience as an undergraduate. Our "Last of the River Rats" course, featuring authentic (and colorful) riverman Kenny Salwey, has been very popular. *First lesson for success: Find faculty and facilitators who are inspiring, creative, and dedicated to the themes they are supporting in the LLCs and who are familiar with the issues that face FGS's (such as isolation, lack of familiarity in managing both with human and technological systems, academic difficulty, cultural incongruities, etc.).*

Some of these courses and themes have been so appealing to students that they have attracted students from beyond the first-year/Residential College experience. *Second lesson for success: Let the rest of the campus know what you are doing; older students can be an even more interested and involved group than FGS's. Which leads to lesson for success #3: Allow older students to continue participating in the LLC process (TA positions were created to allow students to continue with the program after their first year). And also to lesson for success #4: Use the campus recruitment process to recruit FGS's (the concept of residential LLCs is even less familiar to FGS's and their families, who require a first-hand look at the setting and a chance to meet with faculty, and are often impressed by the West Campus's more traditional/British look; our LLC enrollment increased significantly when the residential West Campus began to be included as a regular part of our campus tour).*

Author Katherine E. Chaddock commented in a 2008 publication by the National Resource Center for the First-Year Experience and Students in Transition that college residential life programs have been characterized in the past by "inaction, hopeful experiments, accidental successes, financial barriers, leadership reluctance, leadership enthusiasm"—but that more recently, we have seen an increase in "deliberate endeavors that build on collective evidence of favorable results" (p. 7). We are hopeful that our contribution to this FGS reader will become part of that growing collection and discussion of best practices.

References

Chaddock, K.E. (2008). From inventions of necessity to necessary invention: The evolution of learning in residential settings. In G. Luna & J. Gahagan (Eds.), *Learning initiatives in the residential setting* (Monograph No. 48, pp. 7-17). Columbia, SC: University of South Carolina, National Resource Center for the First-Year Experience and Students in Transition.

First in the Family (n/d). Ready to learn. No way to go. Retrieved June 18, 2009 from the First in the Family website at http://www.firstinthefamily.org/toObama/about_us.html

Fuller, D. (2008, September 16). UC opens classes with record enrollment and brightest freshman class. Retrieved June 18, 2009 from the University of Cincinnati website at http://www.uc.edu/News/NR.aspx?ID+8849

Inkelas, K., Vogt, K., Longerbeam, S., Owen, J., & Johnson, D. (2006). Measuring outcomes of living-learning programs: Examining college environments and student learning and development [Electronic Version]. *The Journal of General Education, 55, 1*, 40-76.

Kuh, G., & Zhao, C. (2004) Adding value: Learning communities and student engagement [Electronic Version]. *Research in Higher Education, 45, 2*, 115-138.

Lopez, A., Merkouris, T., & Olcott, S. (2008, May). A study of the student experience at the Residential College—Final report. Paper presented at the 2008 ACUHO-I LivingLearning Programs Conference, Dallas, TX.

Minkler, J. (2002). Learning communities at the community college [Electronic Version]. *Community College Review,* 7-9.

Pascarella, E., Terenzini, P., & Bliming, G. (1994). The impact of residential life on students. In C. C. Schroeder & P. Marble and Associates (Eds.), *Realizing the educational potential of residence halls* (pp. 22-52). San Francisco, CA: Jossey-Bass.

Pasque, P., & Murphy, R. (2005) Intersections of living-learning programs and social identity as factors of academic achievement and intellectual engagement [Electronic Version]. *Journal of College Student Development*, 2-4.

Smith, B. (2003). Learning communities and liberal education [Electronic Version]. *Academe*, 2.

The Policy Center on the First Year of College (2002). Findings: Second National Survey of First-Year Academic Practices 2002. Retrieved September 5, 2008 from http://www.firstyear.org/survey/survey2002/pdf/q10.pdf

Thayer, P. B. (2000). Retention of students from first generation and low income backgrounds. Opportunity Outlook, pp. 2-8. Retrieved August 31, 2009 from ERIC database, DOI: EJ616662.

Tinto, V. (1998). Colleges as communities: Taking research on student persistence seriously. *The Review of Higher Education*, 21(2), 167-177. Washington Center for Improving the Quality of Undergraduate Education (n/a).

Learning Communities National Resource Center. Retrieved August 27, 2008 from http://www.evergreen.edu/washcenter/lcfaq.htm.

Appendix A: Both Parents Have ONLY a HIGH SCHOOL Education (HS graduate or Below)

New Entering Freshmen Year Term		Frequency	Percent
Fall 2004	Both No Data	181	11.5
	Either No Data	7	.4
	Both parent has a high school education or below	**180**	**11.4**
	One of Parents has Higher degree than High school degree	356	22.6
	Both Parents has a high school education or higher	854	54.1
	Total	1578	100.0
Fall 2005	Both No Data	140	8.1
	Either No Data	13	.7
	Both parent has a high school education or below	**193**	**11.2**
	One of Parents has Higher degree than High school degree	441	25.5
	Both Parents has a high school education or higher	940	54.4
	Total	1727	100.0
Fall 2006	Both No Data	171	9.8
	Either No Data	8	.4
	Both parent has a high school education or below	**195**	**11.2**
	One of Parents has Higher degree than High school degree	423	24.3
	Both Parents has a high school education or higher	942	54.2
	Total	1739	100.0
Fall 2007	Both No Data	173	10.0
	Either No Data	13	.7
	Both parent has a high school education or below	**170**	**9.8**
	One of Parents has Higher degree than High school degree	393	22.7
	Both Parents has a high school education or higher	986	56.8
	Total	1735	100.0

Source: WSU Assessment and Institutional Research Department Background Information Survey (Question 14 and 15), New Entering Freshmen Cohort Table

Appendix B: Focus Group Discussion Questions

Opening Question: Where are you from?

1. In what ways are you involved/or have been involved in your hall or on west campus?

2. What activities have you liked best?

3. Have you seen faculty/staff at any activities you have been involved in?

4. Have you taken a class on west campus or connected with the Residential College?

   If you have taken classes, what was your experience?

5. How is living in the hall an academic experience for you?

6. How is living in the hall a social experience for you?

7. What do you like the least about living on West Campus?

8. What do you like the most about living on West Campus?

9. What changes would you like to see on West Campus?

Appendix C: End of the Year Survey of West Campus Students

Please take a few minutes to take this survey about your experience on the West Campus. Before you take this survey, try to recall all of the activities, clubs, floor programs, coffeehouses and speakers you have attended this year. This study is designed to study the engagement and satisfaction of students on the West Campus. Participation will require approximately **5 minutes**. There are no appreciable risks or benefits from participating in this study. No identifying information will be collected. Participating is voluntary and you may stop participating at any time. If you agree to participate, responding to the questions constitutes your consent. If you have any questions, contact Sarah Olcott at 507-457-2516 or the Human Protections Administrator Nancy Kay Peterson at 507-457-5519.

With what frequency do you...

Circle Appropriate # 1-Never 2-Infrequently 3-Sometimes 4-Frequently 5-Very Frequently

Participate in out of classroom experiences with faculty (fieldtrips, speakers, projects)

Attend educational speakers, seminars, movie or retreats on West Campus.

Interact with faculty outside of the classroom

Interact with staff outside the classrooms (Resident Assistants, Hall Directors, etc)

Talk to others about what you are learning in your classes(student, faculty, family, etc)

Work with faculty and staff on committees, clubs or programs outside of classroom activities.

Participate in study groups with other residents on West Campus

Work with other students on group projects connected with a class

Participate in community service

Use lounges to relax or hang out on West Campus

Socialize with other students on West campus

Attend West Campus activities such as winter formal, Mugshots, condom bingo, etc.

Attend floor activities

Attend Hall Council

How satisfied are you with...
Circle Appropriate # 1-N/A 2-Very dissatisfied 3-Dissatisfied 4-Satisfied 5-Very Satisfied

The educational activities on West Campus (speakers, workshops, retreats, etc.)

Your floor activities

West Campus-wide activities such as winter formal, Mugshots, condom bingo, etc.

Your interactions with other students on West Campus

Your interactions with faculty on West Campus

Your interactions with staff on West Campus (Resident Assistants, Hall Directors, etc)

Your ability to study and get work done on the West Campus

Your ability to socialize on West Campus.

The overall experience living on West Campus

Mark an X in the appropriate space

Gender:
( ) Male ( ) Female

Class Rank:
( ) First- year ( ) Sophomore ( ) Junior ( ) Senior or 5th year

Were you in a Living & Learning Community Fall 2007?
( ) YES ( ) NO

If YES which one?
( ) Curiosity: The Essence of Science
( ) Entrepreneurship
( ) Explorations: Career and Life Choices
( ) Gender and Culture
( ) Global Village
( ) Mississippi River
( ) Native Pathways
( ) Whose Planet it is Anyway?

Appendix D: Data From Student Survey—
Mean Comparisons on Engagement Statements Between LLC
and Non-LLC Students

Engagement Statement	Mean (Overall)	Mean(LLC Students)	Mean (Non-LLC)
Participate in out of classroom experiences with faculty (fieldtrips, speakers, projects)	2.18	2.55	2.03
Attend educational speakers, seminars, movie or retreats on West Campus.	2.11	2.42	1.98
Interact with faculty outside of the classroom	2.57	2.63	2.54
Interact with staff outside the classrooms (Resident Assistants, Hall Directors, etc)	2.74	2.84	2.69
Talk to others about what you are learning in your classes(student, faculty, family, etc)	3.66	3.68	3.65
Work with faculty and staff on committees, clubs or programs outside of classroom activities.	2.27	2.42	2.2
Participate in study groups with other residents on West Campus	2.38	2.45	2.36
Work with other students on group projects connected with a class	3.15	3.14	3.15
Participate in community service	2.3	2.35	2.28
Use lounges to relax or hang out on West Campus	3.01	3.25	2.92
Socialize with other students on West campus	4.23	4.32	4.2
Attend West Campus activities such as winter formal, Mugshots, condom bingo, etc.	2.66	2.87	2.57
Attend floor activities	2.62	2.81	2.55
Attend Hall Council	1.47	1.76	1.36

Appendix E: Data From Student Survey—
Mean Comparisons on Satisfaction Statements Between LLC
and Non-LLC Students

Satisfaction Statements	Mean (Overall)	Mean (LLC Students)	Mean (Non-LLC Students)
The educational activities on West Campus (speakers, workshops, retreats, presentations, etc)	2.79	3.06	2.69
Your floor activities	3.42	3.59	3.35
West Campus wide activities such as winter formal, Mugshots, condom bingo, etc.	3.35	3.5	3.3
With your interactions with other students on West campus	4.15	4.27	4.11
With your interactions with faculty on West Campus	3.18	3.59	3.01
With your interactions with staff on West Campus (Resident Assistants, Hall Directors, etc)	3.6	3.71	3.56
Your ability to study and get work done on the West Campus	3.84	3.87	3.82
Your ability to socialize on West Campus.	4.22	4.26	4.2
With overall experience living on West Campus	4.12	4.17	4.1
With your overall experience this year at WSU	4.18	4.21	4.17

[1] Students who live on West Campus (Residential College) have the opportunity to take part in Living and Learning Communities, Residential Houses, University Studies classes in their hall and live 13 blocks from WSU's main campus.

◆ CHAPTER NINE ◆
THE NINE NEEDS OF LOWER-INCOME, FIRST-GENERATION COLLEGE STUDENTS

Charlie Johnson

I come from the "wrong side of the tracks" in a rustbelt town on the decline from the effects of a changing economy. This is a place in which one is considered lucky to be employed. A factory floor or the cab of a dump truck is one's office. Jobs (not careers or positions) are often days or nights (or both) of monotonous toil. My parents are not college graduates. My mother is disabled. My father works in a factory. He comes home dirty and tired. He has no efficacy at work. He sweats so others can think and decide.

From the age of thirteen I have been a worker as well. But as a college student, I am expected to perform as if I never learned to be a worker, as if I was prepared by professional parents to be a professional myself, as if I went to a school with an ethos of professional expectations. However, my schoolwork was mechanical, routine, and denied its students creativity and control. Teachers tracked me into vocational education. Authoritarian administrators and clanging bells prepared me for a factory future.

Now as I try to find my way through the maze called college, constantly feeling like everyone is referring to some experience that I haven't had, I ask myself questions. Can I shake this inherent self-doubt? Can I overcome my anxiety about speaking in class? Can I really be accepted among these future professionals and decision makers who are the sons and daughters of professionals and decision makers? Or am I relegated to being a pretender who builds a fragile facade of belonging? Does everyone feel as though all eyes are on them waiting for that inattentive moment when they will reveal themselves?

Twenty Years On

I wrote the previous reflection when I was well into my college career. Now, twenty years later, I work with students who are experiencing the same journey, the same struggle, and the same transition I faced two decades ago. My inquiry has focused on answering questions about the success of students from backgrounds like mine. What accounts for the success of students who are able to overcome and transcend lower-income, first-generation backgrounds and find success in college? How does this occur and can it be taught to others? My tentative answers to these questions come from an interdisciplinary study of the foundations of education, and through practice while directing programs aimed at supporting the success of students who face the greatest barriers to success.

Central to this work is hope and idealism. When we imagine something different and more hopeful than what is and work to make it a reality, we are able to test old assumptions and open up space to discover new possibilities that previously seemed improbable. As Aldous Huxley (1962) put it, though we may not succeed in making the "best of all worlds, but by dint of boldly trying" we might make "the best of many more worlds than any merely prudent or sensible person would have dreamed of. . ."

According to Deonandan, Campbell, Ostbye, and Tummon (as cited in Barratt, 2009), socioeconomic status (SES) is a combination of an individual's occupational prestige and educational attainment. FGS "have a lower SES than second-generation students because of their families' educational attainment" (Barratt, 2009). While there are certainly instances of first-generation college students who are not from lower SES backgrounds and students from lower SES backgrounds who are not the first in their family to attend college, I will focus on the fairly inclusive intersection of the two and refer to them as lower-income, first-generation (LIFG) college students.

Most programs charged with the mission of student success for LIFG students focus on access through financial aid and retention through traditional academic support such as workshops and tutoring programs. What I have found is that while sufficient funding and traditional academic support are necessary, it is not near enough. The fact that LIFG students have less money with which to pay the college bill and to support themselves while in college is not the only explanation for the strong relationship between socioeconomic status and academic success. Nor can we sufficiently explain the SES–academic success correlation with the fact that LIFG students are generally less prepared for college than students from higher SES backgrounds. If being lower SES is the degree to which one does without certain resources, then we must look at *all* the resources that these students do without or of which they have less (Payne, 1998). In addition to having relatively fewer financial and academic resources, LIFG students often come from backgrounds with different cultural values and expectations that move against college success. These students also have different social networks of trust, solidarity, and reciprocity. At higher levels of SES, these expectations and networks bestow all kinds of advantages associated with student success.

Consider the point made in a research report on work colleges funded by the Lumina Foundation:

> Work colleges remove financial barriers to access and provide a rich variety of student support services, but it is unclear whether these efforts are able to alleviate differences in social capital that affect educational achievement and subsequent social stratification. (Raps & Jacobs, 2005)

Work colleges have a very long history of supporting the success of LIFG students. Institutions where historically underserved students work on campus to defray the cost of attending college, work colleges know how significant social capital (what you gain and what you can potentially get from social networks) is to the success of their students who lack the kind of social capital associated with college and professional success. LIFG students do not have the benefit of networks of family, friends, and others who have experiences with college success. Their networks are "tuned" to succeed in lower SES environments and not calibrated for success on a college campus.

As captured in my earlier reflection, LIFG students must not only catch up in terms of these social resources, but they must make sometimes painful transitions to the middle-class culture of the college institution. One's cultural background and social networks are sources of identity. The identity of the first-generation college student is threatened in the college environment usually populated by students whose financial, academic, cultural, and social resources are geared toward college success. This experience can reinforce, as it did for me 20 years ago, self-doubt and alienation.

Here is another reflection from my journal, this time as a graduate student:

> I had to recreate myself. I learned to record over my "background characteristics" and "family legacy," which are tickets to perpetuating the past, back to the ranks of the working poor. The resulting growth comes with the pain of alienation, of belonging to neither my working-poor past nor this college culture that brings the suburban and the exurban to the campus. It was and often still is like swimming against the current of a swollen river. (Johnson, 1993)

My expectations of myself, indeed my identity, were formed in the context of the cultures I inhabited. One of those was the culture of a blue-collar, working-poor family and community. The other culture is the dominant culture. I experienced alienation as I internalized the narratives of the dominant culture about myself and the working-poor world to which I belonged. The narratives of meritocracy and hyper-individualism preach that talent, hard work, and sacrifice are the ingredients of success. The meritocratic and rags-to-riches myths regard intelligence and individual effort as the main sources of successful life outcomes while glossing over the powerful economic, social, and cultural forces and historical legacies that shape us. The way I experienced these narratives was reflexive—if I worked hard and sacrificed but did not succeed, I did not have talent or intelligence. If I was a smart kid but did not succeed, I was an underachiever. Success or lack thereof could not be explained any other way in the dominant culture.

As a first-year student, alienation that results from internalizing these measures of one's self becomes a frequent source of anxiety. As much as I wanted something more in life, I also wanted to escape the discomfort and uneasiness of not fitting in and of the daily reminders of where I "belonged" on the social ladder.

Such uneasiness is just the beginning of a transitional challenge for LIFG students. In addition to bringing their marginalization and alienation with them to the campus, LIFG students, if they are to be successful, must find ways to make what is often a painful transition to a middle-class institution that has the tendency to reinforce these internalized societal messages. If they are successful enough with this transition, they find themselves in the emotional hinterland between two worlds—the one they come from and the middle-class world of the institution. This middle stage of the transition is one of tremendous growth, considerable confusion, and emotional challenge. LIFG students experience an internal reorganization of their sense of the world and their place in it as a dual alienation—no longer belonging to home, but not quite belonging to the middle-class world either.

Armed with a better understanding of the relationships between fewer resources of *all* kinds and college success, what do LIFG students need to be successful and to produce life outcomes on par with their advantaged peers? What if we could facilitate the kind of growth and transformation that allows new students to overcome or transcend their limiting circumstances? What if we could facilitate students' development of social capital that unleashes the potential of those marginalized by class and often by other social factors that leads to the kind of "brain gain" that will immeasurably benefit our communities and our changing economy? What if we could support students in ways that will help them successfully navigate the transition from a lower-income background to a middle-class institution?

The Nine Needs of LIFG Students

For some time now, higher education researchers and administrators have been focusing on the first year as a "critical time of transition" for traditional college students. The research suggests that we can be intentional about designing a first-year experience that helps students make this transition successfully (Skipper, 2005). LIFG students face these same first-year challenges to persistence and success. However, as I have discussed, they do so with fewer resources of all kinds. LIFG students must also reconcile the world they come from to this new world in which they have landed. As I suggest in the following section, we can also be intentional about supporting the success of LIFG students. We can do so by closing the resource gaps between LIFG and more advantaged students and meeting their needs beyond adequate financial aid and traditional academic support.

1. *A Road Map for Success*

The German philosophers Heidegger (1977) and Nietzsche (1954) both wrote that we are "thrown into the world." As human beings, we have inherited a world we had no role in making. Yet, we must exist in it, and we hope to thrive in it. Similarly, LIFG students are thrown into the world of college, usually without any instructions for being successful in it. Students from higher-income backgrounds whose parents attended college are likely to have a pretty adequate map for college success. The map was developed over 18 years of life experience with parents, family, friends, community, and typically a schooling experience that prepared them for a place that, while different from high school, is likely to be very familiar to them in terms of its culture, values, and expectations. In short, it is part of the world they come from. Their map (which, no doubt, varies widely from individual to individual) is a representation of a land similar to the one they have traversed their whole lives.

The LIFG map is a different story. These students are lucky if the map says "you should go to college." Their map is likely to be vacant of directional orientation, of topographical features, of the main thoroughfares to success, and, most critically, devoid of the mileposts that measure progress toward one's destination.

In the book *StrengthsQuest*, Clifton and Anderson (2001) note that "research indicates that top achievers tend to set goals *slightly above* their current level of performance, whereas low achievers often set very, very high goals." For Clifton and Anderson, this is evidence for focusing on developing strengths instead of shoring up deficits. When these low achievers are LIFG students, an additional variable may be that they do not have a map that charts the incremental steps or the short-term and intermediate goals so necessary to getting somewhere. They have been inspired to set very big goals, but they do not know how to get there in terms of what to do the first week, the first month, or the first semester of their college career. Instead, they take it day by day, hoping to figure it out before it is too late.

2. A Guide (well, actually guides)

In addition to a map for success, LIFG students also need a guide to this heretofore unknown world, a college success veteran to help them navigate the institution in the pursuit of their goals. Such a college success veteran can help the student "fill in" the map of success. Just as importantly, this guide to the institution can facilitate the student engagement to the campus and the life of university in ways that build social capital for college success. Of course, not one person is likely to be able to meet all the needs of a LIFG student. They need life coaches, mentors, and advocates with expertise to meet a variety of needs. The LIFG student is likely to need multiple guides who have navigated and succeeded in the college environment (Johnson-Bailey & Cervero, 2004).

Given that LIFG students are making a cultural transition to a middle-class college campus, they need guides who have experienced the "dual socialization" characteristic of students in the middle of the transition. I continue to consider myself a denizen of two worlds— my working-poor past, which is still with me, and the middle-class world of higher education that I now inhabit. There is great value, as is often suggested by research on multicultural education, in involving practitioners who are from underrepresented backgrounds who can serve as "cultural translators, mediators, and role models" in building campus support networks that support LIFG students (Rendón, Jalomo, & Nora, 2000).

Our campuses suffer no shortage of college success gurus. However, LIFG students are less likely as strangers in a strange land to make meaningful connections with those in the institution who can guide them. We must be intentional about how to create real relationships between students and their guides.

3. Someone "There" at Attrition/Retention Points

Have you ever felt like giving up on something when it was not going well? Or maybe you have felt like you did not belong at some point in your life. How did feeling low about yourself and the way things were going affect your decision making? We all have experience with life's ebbs. Oftentimes, it was a friend, a family member, or someone else who cared about us who was "there" for us when we needed someone to be "there" most. If we were lucky, that person also had some wisdom to impart that helped us through this low period without us making a bad or costly decision. We were lucky, weren't we?

Who can serve in this role for the LIFG student? Who is "there" when students are at a crisis point when they may very well decide, "That's it, I am quitting!" or "If I needed more proof that I don't belong here, I got it today." Guides, who should be part of the LIFG support network, can help LIFG students develop maps for success and other navigational aids helpful in making transitions to college. Guides can be "there" at these critical times. But how can we increase the likelihood that they will? What is our best hope for getting the student who is facing an attrition/retention point to see the advice we provide as applicable to them? How can we encourage students to follow through on the prescription for resolving whatever issues are behind this low point? These are the questions that must be answered by those serious about enhancing LIFG student success.

One way to ensure that the LIFG student has someone "there" at the right times is the intrusive model of guidance. Earl (1988) describes the model as one that is "action-oriented to involving and motivating students to seek help when needed and is a direct response to an identified academic crisis with a specific program of action." For our LIFG students, the intrusive model manifests itself in a particular way. A guide builds a mentoring relationship with the student that promotes trust and hope. The guide works with the student to develop a plan for success and coaches the student through that plan, mutually modifying the plan with the student as it dynamically plays out. If the student experiences an academic crisis or a life circumstance that impacts academic success, the guide is there as a trusted part of the student's success network to help the student find the campus or community resources necessary to resolve whatever issues he or she is facing.

4. Campus and Community Resources

In the movie *Field of Dreams*, the main character is moved by mystical forces to build a baseball diamond in the middle of an Iowa cornfield. He hears whispers: "if you build it, they will come." True to the whisperer's word, baseball legends emerge from the rows of corn and begin to play ball.

This may work for a fictional baseball field, but not for a campus. If you have spent any time around a college campus, you know that this is not the experience of those who run our academic support resources. Those for whom the support is largely designed stay away because they do not have a success map or a guide who is "there" to direct them to what they need when they need it most. LIFG students need the use of campus and community resources integrated into their success map; they need to be assertively plugged into these services by guides who are "there" as needs arise.

This need is brought into high relief when we look through the lens of social and cultural capital. The LIFG student's social capital, the value that comes from their networks of trust, solidarity and reciprocity (Putnam, 2000; Fukuyama, 1996), by definition does not provide information about what support exists in the college environment. Indeed, utilizing their existing networks can lead away from the institution altogether. If things are not going well, the answer from home might be, "you gave college a try" or "you made it further than anyone else in our family." The message from well-meaning parents of LIFG students can be that some college is better than no college, so it is acceptable to come home. Occasionally, a parent can even feel threatened by the student's college education and be unconsciously motivated to undermine their child's success (Hsiao, 1992).

LIFG students not only need to be engaged in the life of the institution, but they also need to be assertively plugged into campus and community services as needs arise and to have guides and mentors be intrusive with follow up.

5. Know Your Strengths, Values, and Passions

In my early college days when I picked up a tattered and yellowed copy of Viktor Frankl's *Man's Search for Meaning* (1946), I intuitively sensed the significance of the book. I had long been interested in the wisdom of individuals who had overcome or transcended great adversity. Frankl and other thinkers I encountered as an undergraduate helped me begin to explore the tremendous insight and positive power of guiding students to focus on purpose, meaning, and direction as well as what Cooperrider and Srivastva (1987) have called "the good, the better, the true and the possible." These approaches include aiding students in their exploration and discovery of what gives them energy, what gives them hope, and what they truly care about, pushing the boundaries of what is possible and ultimately exploring what makes them unique and how they can give that uniqueness to the world.

I am fond of offering to students some insight borrowed from the philosopher Soren Kierkegaard (1985): we are "constantly in the process of becoming." This happens, day by day, whether we want it to or not. We will be qualitatively different tomorrow and into the future than we are today. We can guide and influence this process with considerable success with knowledge of what drives learning and personal growth and to use those lessons to shape the future you. This is one of the essential principles in helping students reach for their goals, succeed in college, and experience positive life outcomes.

Now imagine how powerful an appreciative, positive, strengths-based approach is with LIFG students who are likely to have internalized all sorts of negative messages about themselves and their backgrounds. The approach turns out be precisely what is needed to help LIFG students examine assumptions about themselves, the world, and their place in it. In doing so, they develop a confidence and optimism grounded in an evolving and more positive sense of self and purpose.

6. Insight that Leads to Resiliency and Emotional Intelligence

Of all the needs delineated here, resiliency and emotional intelligence should be at the top of priority list and are often the ones that campuses are least likely equipped to address. The simple fact is that when we are trying to determine why students succeed or why they fail, we have difficulty accounting for what is probably one of the most salient factors—the students' ability to manage themselves and their emotions.

Why do some students readily bounce back from adversity and others shrink from it and then disappear in defeat? It turns out that we can teach students the elements of resiliency—both those elements within individuals like hope and optimism (see need 5) and those elements that are part of one's networks (see needs 1–3 and 9) (Henderson, Benard, & Sharp-Light, 2007).

It also turns out that we can teach emotional intelligence, which Goleman (1995) tells us includes knowing one's emotions, managing one's emotions, motivating one's self, recognizing emotions in others, and handling relationships. I often think how we all have one foot on the gas and one on the brake, some pressing much harder on the brake than others. I bet right now you have a mental image of someone who fits this description, maybe a student who chronically misses class or procrastinates to the point of failing. Kegan and Lahey (2001) describe the gas and brake as goal commitments and competing commitments. Competing commitments are manifestations of unconscious thoughts that lead to behaviors that impede our efforts to achieve our goals. What is needed is to teach students how to become conscious of their competing commitments and using methods such as those from cognitive behavioral therapy to develop the ability to gradually change patterns of thoughts, feelings, and behaviors that lead one away from success.

There are a whole host of psychosocial-related challenges students face that impact their academic success. LIFG students, tend to face these challenges in greater proportions and often with less support and fewer resources with which to address and cope with these challenges. As we support LIFG students and aid their navigation through the college experience, we also need to pay attention to their emotional needs.

7. Transformative Experiences

During my college career, I learned of the wide array of experiential programs open to students. I found out, for example, one could study just about anywhere in the world. Later I discovered that these programs were mostly accessed by advantaged students. Students with more financial support, more guidance, more familiarity, and more encouragement with these opportunities are, as one might guess, more likely to participate in them and experience tremendous learning and growth as a result. The students with fewer resources, who must work longer hours to pay for college costs, whose family and friends have not studied abroad or participated in other experiential programs, and who might not entertain yet *another* transition like culture shock, are effectively closed off from these kinds of amazing and life-changing experiences.

LIFG student needs these "powerful pedagogies" as much or more than the advantaged student (as cited in Evenbeck and Hamilton, 2006). Twain said "travel is fatal to prejudice, bigotry and narrow-mindedness." I would add that travel can also be fatal to prejudices one has internalized about one's self. Experiential learning of all kinds can help students demystify a world that has so far served to constrain them and define them in negative terms.

Perhaps an even greater reason that LIFG and all nontraditional students merit inclusion in transformative programs is that they have a unique perspective to offer as the result of where they have been "situated" in society prior to attending college, where they are "situated" now as college students. They know the world through a different lens than most students and are able to offer this perspective to the benefit of all. Learning that takes place in classrooms and outside classrooms will be richer as a result of a fuller representation of the diversity of ways of being, seeing, and knowing that exist in the world.

One might be tempted to see it as a luxury, but if we are serious about equitable education, LIFG students need encouragement to explore and equitable access to powerful pedagogies such as undergraduate research, service learning, study abroad, and relevant internships.

8. *Opportunities to Develop Critical Thinking and Intellectual Curiosity*

All students appear to follow a similar path in terms of intellectual development. As Perry (1970) suggests, most beginning students tend see the world in simple dualistic terms. For them, knowledge comes from experts who help us tell the right answers from the wrong answers. LIFG students start from a similar place intellectually. They do not consider themselves capable of having something to say in academic discourse or of pursuing their own questions. LIFG students, however, are less likely to have come from a background that values intellectual development and inquiry. Their cultural capital lends itself more to a vocational approach to education. They are also less likely to have a positive academic self-image.

What can we do to support the intellectual development of LIFG students? The task is to help them make the transition from the banking notion of education where the teacher "deposits" knowledge into the student's brain (Freire, 1970) to one that is based on learning theories that promote interpretation, criticality, inquiry, and discourse. Through teaching critical thinking and encouraging curiosity, we can help students discover that as human beings they share in the creation of knowledge and in shaping the world they inhabit instead of thinking they are passive recipients of knowledge and have no role in creating the future. As Postman (1995) puts it, we can teach them that they are "word weavers and world makers."

9. College and Professional Success Networks

As we have discussed, higher levels of social and cultural capital bestow advantages across the resource spectrum that are associated with student success. Lower-SES students with less of the social and cultural capital associated with college and professional success must not only catch up, but they must make a sometimes painful transition to the middle-class culture of the institution. Possessing less social and cultural capital are also sources of student identity and reinforce self-doubt and alienation. Much of the previous eight needs involve finding ways to develop social and cultural capital for LIFG students that will lead to college and professional success. The remaining needs are focused on encouraging the psychosocial and intellectual development of students so they can realize their human potential for growth and learning.

This ninth need emphasizes the importance of helping students to develop the kind of networks that will lead to success in college. It is a distinct ninth need because it is a key to meeting the previous eight needs in some way or another. Additionally, I include it because it is not enough to promote LIFG students' engagement with the institution in the ways I have described. They also need to learn about these networks themselves and how to develop them.

When I graduated from college with a 4.0 GPA, I fully expected the world to come to me. I thought my academic success would open the doors to professional success. After all, dominant cultural narratives taught me that success began and ended with the individual. I reasoned that I had won at that game. Of course, no one came knocking. I was good at reading critically, writing papers, and taking tests, but I still did not have a clue about how one accesses the professional world.

So what did I do? Well, I tapped into the networks I had. Those in the networks I had developed as an undergraduate suggested that I go to graduate school. Those in the networks I had at home suggested I return to the factories until something else came along. I had no networks that could help me figure out how to develop a map for professional success. I had no networks of people who might be familiar with relevant career opportunities. I certainly knew no one that held a professional position related to my interests that could get me started in a postbaccalaurcate world. I learned personally what I now know professionally, LIFG students need to develop social capital associated with BOTH college success and professional success.

The Struggles of LIFG Students at Middle-Class Institutions
Saufley, Cowan, and Blake (1983) succinctly and comprehensively describe challenges that minority students face as college students. While the historical and structural significance of race and ethnicity cannot and should not be glossed over, many of the challenges they describe are experienced by white and minority students alike who are from lower-income backgrounds and are the first in their families to attend college. These struggles include a lack of hope, negative academic self-image reinforced by isolation and alienation, family pressures, feeling like an imposter in class, a sense of apartness from the "patterns of living around them," and fear of failure that can manifest as procrastination or even a total loss of motivation. These elements in total, the authors assert, leads to a "systematic academic invalidation."

Saufley et al. (1983) conclude that we should recognize the "precarious position" for these students, and "we must be willing to approach the challenge with considerably more sensitivity, insight and willingness to change than we have exhibited in the past." I contend this is also a path to increasing the participation and success of all LIFG students. Meeting the nine needs of LIFG students beyond financial aid and traditional academic support is like a river flowing into valleys of neglect. It is also a tried and tested approach. The Nina Mason Pulliam Legacy Scholars Program, a program I direct at Indiana University-Purdue University Indianapolis has been using elements of this approach for more than eight years. It is a program, funded by the Nina Mason Pulliam Charitable Trust that supports the success the success of lower-income students from foster care backgrounds, who are returning adults with children, or who have physical disabilities. This program has a retention rate of 93%, a graduation rate that has ranged from 70% to 80%, and almost 60% of its graduates are in graduate school or have completed a graduate degree. Amazing things can happen when we focus on what strengths LIFG students bring to campus and what resources they need relative to college and professional success. We can fill the gap between those with greater resources and those with fewer resources in innumerable ways that lead to uncommon success. Rather than continue to reinforce the limitations and constraints that inhibit the success of LIFG students, perhaps our best bet as educators is to create instances and opportunities for these students to get what advantaged students tend to have in more abundance.

References

Barratt, W. (2009). *Socioeconomic status: The inequitable campus*. Retrieved July 27, 2009, from http://wbarratt.indstate.edu/socialclass/acp a2005/default.htm

Bourdieu, P., & Coleman, J. (Eds.). (1991). *Social theory for a changing society*. Boulder, CO: Westview Press.

Clifton, D., & Anderson, E. (2001). *StrengthsQuest: Discover and develop your strengths in academics, career, and beyond*. New York: Gallup Press.

Cooperrider, D. L., & Srivastva, S. (1987). Appreciative inquiry in organizational life. In W. Pasmore & R. Woodman (Eds.), *Research in organization change and development* (Vol. 1). Greenwich, CT: JAI Press.

Earl, W. R. (1988). Intrusive advising for freshmen in academic difficulty. *NACADA Journal, 8*(2), 27–33.

Evenbeck, S., & Hamilton, S. (2006). From "my course" to "our program": Collective responsibility for first-year student success. *Peer Review, 8*(3), 17–19.

Frankl, V. (1946). *Man's search for meaning*. New York: Pocket Books.

Freire, Paulo. (1970). *Pedagogy of the oppressed*. New York: Continuum Publishing

Fukuyama, F. (1996). *Trust: The social virtues and the creation of prosperity*. New York: Simon and Schuster.

Goleman, D. (1995). *Emotional intelligence: Why it can matter more than IQ*. New York: Bantam Books.

Heidegger, M. (1977). *Basic writings*. New York: Harper and Row

Henderson, N., Benard, B., & Sharp-Light, N. (2007). *Resiliency in action: Practical ideas for overcoming risks and building strengths in youth, families, and communities*. Ojai, CA: Resiliency in Action.

Hsiao, K. P. (1992). First-generation college students. *ERIC Clearing house for Junior Colleges*. Los Angeles: Office of Educational Research and Improvement.

Huxley, A. (1962). *Island*. London: Harper and Row.

Johnson, C. (1988). Unpublished journal.

Johnson, C. (1993). Unpublished journal.

Johnson-Bailey, J., & Cervero, R. M. (2004). Mentoring in black and white: The intricacies of cross-cultural mentoring. *Mentoring and Tutoring, 12*(1), 7–21.

Kegan, R., & Lahey, L. L. (2001). *How the way we talk can change the way we work: The seven languages of transformation*. San Francisco: Jossey-Bass.

Kierkegaard, S. (1985). *Philosophical fragments*. (H. V. Hong & E. H. Hong, Trans.). Princeton, NJ: Princeton University Press.

Nietzsche, F. (1954). *The portable Nietzsche*. (W. Kaufmann, Trans.) New York: Viking Press.

Payne, R. K. (1998). *A framework for understanding poverty*. Highlands, TX: Aha! Process.

Perry, W. G., Jr. (1970). *Forms of intellectual and ethical development in the college years*. New York: Holt, Rinehart and Winston.

Postman, N. (1995). *End of education: Redefining the value of school*. New York: Vintage Books.

Putnam, R. D. (2000). *Bowling alone: The collapse and revival of American community*. New York: Simon and Schuster.

Raps, B., & Jacobs, D. (2005, November). *Results of the work colleges consortium collaborative research*. Report to Lumina Foundation for Education. Berea, KY: Work Colleges Consortium.

Rendón, L. I., Jalomo, R. E., & Nora, A. (2000). Theoretical considerations in the study of minority student retention in higher education. In J. M. Braxton (Ed.), *Reworking the student departure puzzle*. Nashville, TN: Vanderbilt University Press.

Saufley, R. W., Cowan, K. O., & Blake, H. J. (1983). The struggles of minority students at predominantly white institutions. *New Directions for Teaching and Learning, 1983*(16), 3–15.

Skipper, T. L. (2005). *Student development in the first college year: A primer for college educators*. Columbia: University of South Carolina, National Resource Center for the First-Year Experience and Students in Transition.

Mark Twain. (n.d.). *Quotes.net*. Retrieved August 30, 2009, from Quotes.net Web site: http://www.quotes.net/quote/1657

• CHAPTER TEN •
CONCLUSIONS

Vickie Harvey and Teresa Heinz Housel

This book has examined how first-generation students are a diverse population with particular, but complex needs that can be addressed through university and college programs. Although low socio-economic status is a characteristic often associated with first generation student (FGS) status, other personal attributes that include ethnicity, race, sexual orientation, geographical origin, age, familial status, and gender factors can influence a student's academic success in similar ways.

The two sections in the book go beyond identifying what we already know about FGS by giving unheard voices an opportunity to be heard and to identify some successful college and university programs. Academic programs that assist FGS become an opportunity for greater student retention, student achievement, and provide a passport for the construction of new professional identities.

In addition to the multi-faceted nature of students' situations, this book's essays point out how educational institutions must develop holistic approaches to ensuring FGS success. Some institutions address lower retention rates among FGS by offering pre-orientation programs that focus on the registration process and financial aid. These programs are important, but they do not address the larger emotional and cultural adjustments to academic culture that FGS must make.

Additionally, too many programs are geared toward traditionally-aged college students. However, these programs are now too narrow in focus to reach the changing college population. The economic recession is leading many unemployed people in unskilled jobs to seek an associate's or bachelor's degree in order to competitively retrain for the new economy. Scholarships, loans, and grant programs have certainly made college attainable for more students who are FGS and nontraditional. Many academic institutions, especially public and state colleges, no longer assume that college students will live on campus or enter college between the ages of 18-21.

Collectively, this book's essays detail best practices for serving FGS. The essays argue that institutions must address financial aid, academic skills (reading, writing, oral communication, and test-taking skills), student living accommodations, class schedules that are flexible enough for working students and those with families, emotional and cultural issues, and challenges related to ethnicity, race, and sexual orientation.

When attention is especially paid to first generation college students, two central considerations prevail. One consideration holds that the primary purpose of academic institutions concerning FG students, including administrators and faculty, is to prepare FG students for a specialized major; the other, that the purpose of preparation and instruction serves as an antidote to specialization, vocationalism, and majors. Administration hopes that faculty could somehow provide a framework for an inclusive general education, but it is only with the implementation of such resources that supports FGS that faculty can expand their involvement with FGS to better meet the challenges they bring to our campuses.

This book points to valuable topics for future research so that administrators and staff can better ensure FGS success. For example, researchers should consider using diverse methodologies. For example, anthropological research methods are increasingly informing education research. Qualitative methods such as ethnography could help researchers better understand how FGS communicate and navigate their changing identity in the college setting. Other on-the-ground methods such as participant observation could help researchers understand how FGS grapple with academic culture and respond to the often unspoken expectations of faculty and staff.

One of this book's strengths is its offering of creative and innovative quantitative research on the first-generation experience. However, additional quantitative research could provide inside into how non-FGS perceive their first-generation peers and vice versa. Their non-first-generation peers' common stereotypes and assumptions, perceived behaviors, and attitudes form one barrier to academic

AUTHOR INFORMATION

success. A better understanding of these barriers and how they are manifested in peer relations on campus could help faculty more effectively include class issues in discussion and course readings. Additionally, institutions could better include class issues in campus diversity training programs.

FGS bring an important but underrepresented perspective into academia. It is difficult for FGS to receive sometimes unspoken messages about how they won't academically succeed from administrators, faculty, and staff. By recognizing contextual factors such as first-generation status that influence academic performance and cultural transition into college, colleges and universities can create campus environments that are appreciative and respectful of everyone. Many FGS already possess the survival skills and high ability that give them the courage to forge the unfamiliar college path. However, faculty, staff, and administrators can work together to help even more FGS create stories of success. Orbe (2004) emphasizes the importance of such a cohesive unit that is especially critical for FG students' success. Because FGS often lack a sense of community with other FGS, the campus climate offers a greater influence on their academic and professional identity development. When administrators, staff, and faculty work together to better serve FGS, students' college experience allows them to carve their own path toward greater academic and professional achievement.

Reference

Orbe, M. (2004). Negotiating multiple identities within multiple frames: An analysis of first-generation college students. *Communication, 53*(2), 131-149.

◆ AUTHOR INFORMATION ◆

Primary Authors/Editors:
Teresa Heinz Housel and Vickie L. Harvey

Our Qualifications for Editing This Book

Teresa Heinz Housel:

As an assistant professor in Hope College's Communication Department, I am responsible for teaching our introductory to communication course and courses in journalism and cultural studies. My working-class family background lends a practical and empathetic perspective to my teaching and research. I completed my undergraduate education at Oberlin College, an institution attended by many students from upper-class backgrounds. At that time, Oberlin had virtually no support resources for first-generation college students. Because my family had not attended college, I felt as though I could not talk with anyone when faced with decisions about what courses to take; how to strategically study for class; and how to handle the ever-present financial strain of paying for college. Now, as a communication teacher and researcher, I often mentor first-generation college students at Hope who informally talk with me about their struggles. Their important perspectives diversify and enrich our college community.

My class experiences shape my research on class, media, and culture. My master's thesis is the only academic study of the cultural impact of *The Big Issue*, a British magazine sold by homeless people in Britain and Ireland. I studied the British media's portrayals of homelessness, interviewed journalists from all five national British newspapers, and surveyed the journalists to see if *The Big Issue* had caused them to have more sympathy for homeless people. I found that the magazine had led journalists to better understand the complex reasons for homelessness.

For my doctoral dissertation, I examined portrayals of homeless people in *The Washington Post* and *The Christian Science Monitor*. The media tends to individualize homelessness to people's personal shortcomings, rather than examine larger structural causes of homelessness. I concluded that cultural values of hard work, individualism, consumption, and success in American culture also sustain economic stratification.

I am currently completing a co-authored book on social class, *Staging Class: How We Talk About and Live Class in America*, with Dr. Carolyn Calloway-Thomas, associate professor of Communication and Culture and Culture and Adjunct Professor of African American Studies at Indiana University. Our book will be a much-needed update of the communication research on social class in America. Our research covers new ground in social class research by analyzing how class stratification is often erased through the ways people talk about class. As these research projects indicate, I have a keen understanding of class in the United States because I have lived the experience. My edited volume with Vickie Harvey is a natural extension of my understanding of how our class backgrounds shape our identities and experiences.

Vickie L. Harvey:

First-generation college students cross several borders: socio-economic class, nontraditional students, lesbian and gay students, race and ethnic backgrounds, and learning disabled students, just to identify a few. My inclusion in some of the previous categories as a FGS gives me a unique individual perspective. This particular perspective allows me to approach pedagogy and students in ways that ideally best serve them, the classroom environment, and the university at large.

My scholarly record of publishing 12 peer reviewed articles; being a writer and presenter of more than 18 regional, national, and international conference papers; teaching college for 15 years; and serving as a reviewer for two journals *(Western Journal of Communication* and *Women and Language)* demonstrates my dedication to overcoming challenges traditionally associated with FGS and other minority groups.

There is an emerging sense of professional identity that now includes FGS in academic positions. No longer is attending college reserved for the elite or affluent, nor is securing a teaching, research, or administrative position reserved for those whose parents paved the way for them at four-year educational institutions. Now, it is rather the child who paves the way for broader horizons and greater opportunities than afforded to their non-college graduating family members. I had no parent or sibling pave the way or even leave bread crumbs. Instead, I forged on my own through the thick thistles and thorns to emerge as a first-generation college professor.

As I look around at my first-generation colleagues, I now see many of us finding our voices together.

CO-EDITOR INFORMATION

Teresa Heinz Housel, Hope College

Teresa Heinz Housel is an assistant professor of Communication at Hope College in Holland, Michigan. While a first-generation college student at Oberlin College in the early 1990s, she became interested in how the academic environment culturally marginalizes many first-generation students. Her research in the areas of homelessness, the politics of housing, media and globalization, and language, power, and class have appeared in *Critical Studies in Media Communication*, *Information, Communication & Society*, and *Journal of Critical Inquiry*.

Contact Information:
Teresa Heinz Housel, Assistant Professor
Department of Communication
Martha Miller Center, Room 126
Holland, MI 49423
Office Phone: (616) 395-7268
Fax: (616) 395-7937
E-mail: housel@hope.edu

Vickie L. Harvey, California State University, Stanislaus

Vickie Harvey is an associate professor in the Communication Studies Department at the California State University, Stanislaus. She conducts research and teaches courses that emphasize the importance of communicating in relationships. Her primary line of research focuses on cross-sex friendships and how platonic friends meet O'Meara's four challenges of remaining just friends. Her research has been published in *Sex Roles, Communication Teacher, Iowa Journal of Communication, The Qualitative Report, International Journal of Information and Communication Technology Education*, and *Readings in Gender Communication*.

Contact Information:
Vickie L. Harvey, Associate Professor
Department of Communication Studies
California State University, Stanislaus
One University Circle
Turlock, CA 95382
Office Phone: (209) 667-3940
Fax: (209) 667-3525
E-mail: Vharvey@csustan.edu

INFORMATION FOR CONTRIBUTING AUTHORS

Andreas Anastasiou, Mary Baldwin College

Associate Professor Andreas Anastasiou teaches psychology at Mary Baldwin College. He teaches clinical courses as well as the Psychology of Peace and Conflict Resolution and Multicultural Psychology. He earned his Ph.D. in counseling psychology at the University of Pittsburgh. His research interests include art therapy and the role of empathy in conflict resolution. He earned a National Institutes of Health grant to study gender in the communication of empathy toward perceived adversarial groups in collaboration with co-author Alice Araujo.

Contact Information:
Andreas Anastasiou
Associate Professor
Department of Psychology
Mary Baldwin College
Staunton, Virginia 24401
Phone: (540) 887-7109
E-mail: aanastas@mbc.edu

Alice Araujo, Mary Baldwin College

Associate Professor Alice Araujo teaches human communication courses at Mary Baldwin College in Staunton, Virginia. She has earned her Ph.D. in Communication Studies from the University of Kansas and received two grants from the National Institutes of Health to study gender and the communication of empathy toward perceived adversarial groups. In addition, Araujo has worked as a facilitator for the Virginia Foundation of Independent Colleges and for the Associated Colleges of the South Summer Workshops for College Teachers.

Contact Information:
Alice Araujo
Associate Professor
Department of Communication
Mary Baldwin College
Staunton, Virginia 24401
Phone: (540) 887-7019
E-mail: aaraujo@mbc.edu

Ronald J. Elcombe, Winona State University

For the past six years, Ronald J. Elcombe has served as Director of the Winona State University Residential College. In that capacity, he has worked in partnership with the WSU Residence Life department to develop and implement a Living and Learning Community program aimed at the 800+ first and second year students living on the WSU west campus. In addition, Elcombe has been a professor of Mass Communication (Advertising) for nearly 17 years and prior to joining the academy had a successful professional career in advertising and marketing. He believes one of the hallmarks of the success of the WSU Residential College is the collaboration between Academic Affairs and Residence Life, and that there has been a conscious effort on the part of both areas of the university to work together to provide an exciting living and learning experience for first- and second-year students.

Contact Information:

Ronald J. Elcombe
Director, Residential College
Lourdes 152
Winona State University
Winona, Minnesota 55987
Phone: (507) 457-2501
E-mail: RElcombe@winona.edu

Jena Griswold, University of Pennsylvania Law School

Jena Griswold spent the first ten years of her life Toledo, Ohio, before moving to Estes Park, Colorado. The distinct socio-economic cultures of Toledo and Estes Park amazed her, and she slowly began to question the role of class in American culture. Griswold attended Whitman College, where she co-founded the Whitman College Working Class, a coalition of working-class students, faculty, and staff. Then, in 2005-2006, she and Harmony Paulsen were awarded a Mellon Grant to examine socio-economic class at the liberal arts college. After graduation, Griswold researched cultural globalization as a Watson Fellow, worked as a freelance editor, and opened a youth hostel in Colombia. Griswold currently attends the University of Pennsylvania Law School.

Contact Information:

Jena Griswold
201 S. 18th St.

Philadelphia, Pennsylvania 19103
Phone: (970) 214-4889
E-mail: jena.gris@gmail.com

Charlie Johnson, Indiana University-Purdue University Indianapolis (IUPUI)

Charlie Johnson is the Director of Scholar Support Programs at IUPUI in Indianapolis, Indiana. He serves as the Director of the Nina Mason Pulliam Legacy Scholars Program, which supports the success of students who have been wards of the court, who have physical disabilities, or are low-income adults with children. He also provides leadership for the post-secondary support of Twenty-first Scholars at IUPUI and throughout Indiana. The Twenty first Century Scholars Program is designed to raise the aspirations and support the success of low- and moderate-income families in Indiana. Johnson also teaches courses in Critical Inquiry and Mentoring at IUPUI. Johnson has served in a variety of academic positions at Indiana University, Texas A&M University, and IUPUI. Johnson received his M.S. in Foundations of Education from Indiana University and a B.S. in English and Humanities from Ball State University. He resides in Westfield, Indiana with his wife, Julie, and their three children, Alex, Annie, and Drew.

Contact Information:
Charlie Johnson
Director of Scholar Support Programs
Nina Mason Pulliam Legacy Scholars Program
IUPUI University College
UC B10 C
Indianapolis, Indiana 46202
Phone: (317) 278-7878
E-mail: chajohns@iupui.edu

Brandi Lawless, University of New Mexico

Brandi Lawless received her B.A. in Communication Studies in 2003 from California State University, Northridge and her M.A. from San Francisco State University. She is currently pursuing her Ph.D. in Communication at the University of New Mexico. Though she is not a first-generation college student, she does identify with a key characteristic of many who are: lower/working class. While her parents went to college out of necessity, she was a "first-generation" academic. Brandi's current research focuses on the liminality that exists between social classes and its effect on language, perception, and identification. Taking this framework and applying it to personal experiences, recent academic explorations include identifying the communication of classism in higher education.

Contact Information:
Brandi Lawless
Department of Communication and Journalism
University of New Mexico
MSC03 2240, Albuquerque, NM 87131-0001
Phone: (505) 277-5305
E-mail: blawless@unm.edu

Keith Nainby, California State University
Dr. Keith Nainby is Assistant Professor of Communication Studies at California State University, Stanislaus. A first–generation student himself, his research interests include communication pedagogy, performance–based pedagogy and performances of social class. He earned his doctorate, specializing in Philosophy of Communication, from Southern Illinois University, Carbondale in 2003.

Contact Information:
Keith Nainby
Department of Communication Studies
Demergasso Bava-Hall Building
One University Circle
California State University, Stanislaus
Turlock, California 95382
Phone: (209) 667-3523
E-mail: KNainby@stan.csustan.edu

Sarah Olcott, Winona State University
Sarah Olcott received her M.Ed. from the University at Buffalo in College Student Services and Development and her B.S in English from the State University of New York at Geneseo. She worked in Residence Life for seven years before taking her current position as Program Coordinator at the Residential College at Winona State University. Olcott has been working in residential living and learning initiatives for the past eight years at two universities. As a Hall Director, she worked to establish the relationship between housing and

the academic programs of the Residential College. She continues to assist first year students by providing assistance to nine Living and Learning Communities and works with faculty to make those transitional programs a success. She believes that Living and Learning Communities help to transition the first year student to college life by connecting them to a faculty member who is interested in them and shares an interest in an academic area. Olcott hopes that first generation students can especially benefit from these programs. She is the direct supervisor for the Mugshots West Campus coffeehouse and works with the two student coordinators as well as the Entrepreneurship Living and Learning Community.

Contact Information:
Sarah Olcott, Program Coordinator
Residential College
Lourdes 129
Winona State University
Winona, Minnesota 55987
Phone: (507) 457-2516
E-mail: SOlcott@winona.edu

Kenneth Oldfield, University of Illinois, Springfield
Kenneth Oldfield is an award-winning author and emeritus professor of public administration at the University of Illinois at Springfield. Neither of his parents and none of his grandparents finished high school, and all held blue-collar jobs. Oldfield's grandmother, who was a cook in a "greasy spoon restaurant," raised him. He has published articles on various topics including property tax administration, Graduate Record Examination predictive validity, the Office of Economic Opportunity, personnel selection and orientation, community college funding disparities, property-assessment uniformity, tax increment financing, the human genome project, graduate internships, the philosophy of science, and the sociology of knowledge. More recently, Oldfield has been researching, publishing papers, and making conference and keynote presentations about democratizing higher education through use of socio-economic-based affirmative action to recruit and place more college students and professors of poverty and working-class origins.

Contact Information:
Kenneth Oldfield
Emeritus Professor of Public Administration

University of Illinois at Springfield
2125 Kenwood Ave.
Springfield, Illinois 62704-4325
Phone: (217) 546-0772
E-mail: oldfield.ken@uis.edu

Harmony Paulsen

Harmony Paulsen was the co-president of a Working Class support and advocacy group at Whitman College in Walla Walla, Washington, where she helped to create a supportive campus community for working class students, staff and faculty. As a first-generation college student from a low-income household, Harmony worked her way through school and graduated in 2006 with an honors degree in Politics and Environmental Studies. She currently works as project management consultant on environmental remediation projects at contaminated federal facilities. She will pursue a graduate degree in water policy and management in the fall of 2010.

Contact Information:
Harmony Paulsen
Whitman College Alumnae
P.O. Box 1687
Seattle, Washington 98103
Phone: (206) 730-3746
E-mail: harmonysimone@gmail.com

JoAnne M. Podis

JoAnne M. Podis is Vice President for Academic Affairs and Professor of English at Ursuline College in Ohio. She is the co-author of three textbooks on writing and has presented and published consistently over a thirty-year career in private higher education. Her most recent publication is the lead article in the November 2007 issue of *College English*, co authored with Leonard A. Podis. Her teaching and research interests, in addition to writing pedagogy, include women in popular culture, world cinema, and Jane Austen. The daughter of working-class Bohemian immigrants, in recent years she has begun constructing her literacy narrative as part of a series of panels presented at the Conference on College Communication and Composition.

Contact Information:
JoAnne M. Podis
Vice President for Academic Affairs and Professor of English
Ursuline College, Mullen 322
Pepper Pike, Ohio 44124
Phone: (440) 646-8107
E-mail: jpodis@ursuline.edu

Rita L. Rahoi-Gilchrest, Winona State University

Rita L. Rahoi-Gilchrest, Ph.D. (Ohio University) is Associate Professor/Department Chair in Communication Studies at Winona State University, Winona, Minnesota. She has taught in the Midwest as well as in Oslo, Norway, and Christchurch, New Zealand in communications and marketing, and had a decade of experience in both public and commercial broadcasting prior to entering academia. Her direct experience working with first-generation college students currently comes through teaching the required basic skills course in Public Speaking as well as through teaching sections of Winona State University's one-credit orientation/Introduction to Higher Education class. She has also taught and mentored first-generation college students at Ohio University and the University of Missouri-St. Louis. Rahoi-Gilchrest's work has been published in *Communication Quarterly*, the *Howard Journal of Communication, Gazette*, and numerous regional journals as well as in several edited book chapters. She researches and consults in organizational rhetoric, crisis communication, and diffusion of innovations, and is herself a first-generation college student and a proud half-Swedish granddaughter of Wisconsin immigrants from Sweden's Varmland region.

Contact Information:
Rita L. Rahoi-Gilchrest, Professor
Department Chair, Communication Studies Department
Winona State University
Performing Arts Center 204
Winona, Minnesota 55987
Phone: (507) 457-2362